Journey Through the Feasts of the Lord

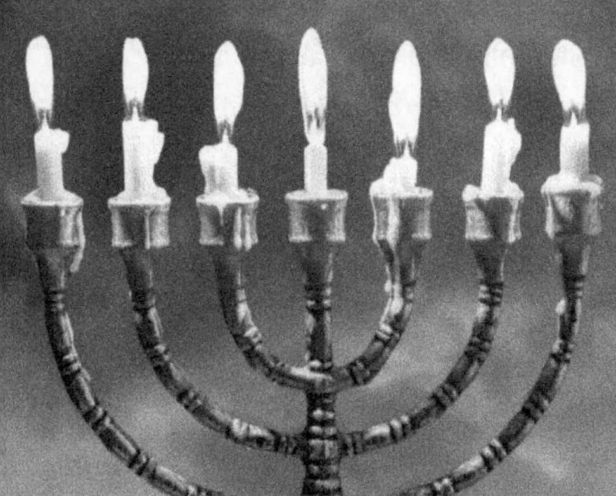

Fred Stapleton

Journey Through the Feasts of the Lord

ISBN: 978-1-964359-27-4

Address all personal correspondence to:

Fred Stapleton: *freddiestapleton12@gmail.com*

Connie Stapleton: *conniestapl@aol.com*

Author Website: *https://www.ccworldmissions.org*

Artwork & Illustrations by Sasha Beach

Individuals and church groups may order books from Fred Stapleton directly, or from the publisher. Retailers and wholesalers should order from our distributors. Refer to the Deeper Revelation Books website for distribution information, as well as an online catalog of all our books.

Published by:

Deeper Revelation Books
Revealing "the deep things of God" (1 Cor. 2:10)
P.O. Box 4260
Cleveland, TN 37320 423-478-2843
Website: *www.deeperrevelationbooks.org*
Email: *info@deeperrevelationbooks.org*

Deeper Revelation Books assists Christian authors in publishing and distributing their books. Final responsibility for design, content, permissions, editorial accuracy, and doctrinal views, either expressed or implied, belongs to the author.

If your desire is to know a depth of Christ in a way not previously known, and in reality, cannot be known from a casual reading of the Bible, you hold in your hands a book that unlocks the depths of the inexhaustible riches of Christ. Pastor Fred Stapleton has an understanding and revelation of the Feasts of the Lord that, I believe, is unparalleled in our day. His love for the rich history of the People of God and the Word of God given through them has brought him wonderful insights into the Feasts (appointed times, *Moedim*, Holy Convocations) of the Lord. I encourage you to have your Bible at hand and allow the Spirit of God to bring enlightenment to your understanding as you read this wonderful book.

Pastor Scott Adams
Living Word Ministries, Chesterfield, SC

This book is one of the most inspiring books I've read pertaining to the Feasts of the Lord. It is an eye-opening read with depth into the Scriptures and the before knowing plans of God. This is a must read, and hard to put down once you have started. Enjoy.

Pastor Glenn White
Lighthouse Ministries, Hartsville, SC

I am so honored for the privilege of working with my dad on his book, *Journey Through the Feasts of the Lord*. This book really dives into the meaning of each feast and will give you a clear understanding of each one. I was so amazed as I worked with him on this book on how it went right along with the Word of God.

Joy Danielle Boyd
Secretary, Cornerstone Covenant World Missions, Granite Falls, NC

It has been my pleasure to know Apostle Freddie for five years. I have not known him exceptionally long, but in Spirit, it feels like I have always known him. I have many acquaintances, but few friends. I consider Apostle Freddie my friend. He is a great partner in the ministry, and I admire his passion for the Lord and for people all over the world. I have had the privilege to travel to Romania and Ukraine with Apostle. He is loved by many. I truly knew that God connected us from the first time that we met. In *Journey Through the Feasts of the Lord*,

Apostle Freddie does an excellent job breaking down all the feasts for the reader to comprehend and get a better understanding. There is an excerpt in his book that sticks out to me on the Mercy Seat. 1 John 2:2—*"And he is the propitiation for our sins: and not for our sins only, but also for the sins of the whole world."* The word propitiation is from the Greek word *hilasterion* which means Mercy Seat. Apostle Freddie is truly knowledgeable on the feasts and wishes to transfer his knowledge through this amazing book. He has a revelation like no other. The anointing of the Holy Ghost rests upon this author, and as you read his amazing book, the anointing and knowledge will be transferred to you. Open your heart and get ready to receive a deeper revelation as you begin to read, *Journey Through the Feasts of the Lord.*

Dr. Bishop Jamie Moore D. Min., M. Christian Education
Founder of New Covenant Christian Center, Flat Rock, AL

Journey Through the Feasts of the Lord has been an outstanding tool for me to learn from a man of God that I truly respect. You don't have to question the teaching in this book because it has supporting Scripture all through out. I look forward to reading each chapter again throughout the year as the feasts are observed. No matter how much I study the Word of God, Dr. Fred Stapleton can always dig something out of the Scripture that I have missed. He is my father in the Lord, and I love and honor his precious family!

Matthew and Jessica Howell
Hands and Feet of Jesus Ministries, Morganton, NC

As I read through the manuscript, it came to me as a servant of God, still pregnant with so much of God after traveling to towns and villages to share the Word of God. I could see Apostle Dr. Freddie Stapleton's desire to open deep revelations about the Feast of the Tabernacle to the world and Christian Community in general. His book confronts issues that pertain to the feast and its celebration and its application to us today. The book also confronts what the feast is all about. One can see Apostle Dr. Freddie Stapleton's rich experience in ministry and well-researched truth about the "FEAST." I hereby sincerely recommend this book to anyone unborn, born-again Christians, and preachers working in the Vineyard of God. His suggested solutions to some of the misconceptions about the feast will be solved.

Apostle John Kwaku Appiah
Ghana, West Africa

Bringing understanding to the Body of Christ is so necessary in this day. I am truly privileged to have such a man of God in my life as Bro. Fred Stapleton. He has studied the Bible for many years. Having read this book, it has brought so much understanding to me through the Feasts of the Lord. Without understanding of these feasts, there is really no understanding of who Jesus really is. Thank you so much for writing this book. I know that many will gain a greater understanding of the Word of God through this message. I highly recommend to anyone that is hungry for knowledge of the feasts to read this book. God bless!

Pastor Stacy Stines
Blueridge Mountain Church, Elk Park, NC

We appreciate Apostle Fred Stapleton for asking my wife Judy and I to endorse his latest book "Journey through the Feast of the Lord". We know he has given himself completely to the understanding of the Feasts of the Lord. As you read this book if you will read it with an open mind and the spirit of the Lord in your heart, you will begin to see the greatness of what God is saying in the Feast of the Lord. Brother Fred Stapleton has always searched out scriptures and has a knowledge of the scripture like no other man of God I know. With a glad heart we endorse this book! We pray you enjoy the revelation of what God is saying in these things. We pray it will be a blessing to you as read this book!

Pastors Danny and Judy Honeycutt
Cornerstone Covenant Church, Hudson, NC

Apostle Fred Stapleton has an expository writing style, guiding the reader in a clear way on how to celebrate Jesus through Biblical feasts. I love that he seeks Christianity's roots in the Jewish tradition and Old Testament. He offers practical advice and Biblical evidence on incorporating Jesus in the Feasts of the Lord into church and family life to enrich our understanding of Jesus and His salvation story. I recommend this book for those who want to understand the Old Testament teachings in light of the New Testament and Jewish tradition. It will truly open your eyes to see how important the Feast of the Lord is to us in our walk with Christ.

Pastor Toby B. Shaw
Co-Vice President of Cornerstone Covenant World Missions
One Love Community Church, Westminster, SC

To the ends of the earth and everywhere in between. I have been blessed to be a part of Cornerstone Covenant Church, where I met Apostle Fred a few years ago, and ever since he has guided me and blessed my family by sharing the Word of the Lord with us. I am so thankful and honored to have been given the opportunity to paint the artwork for his book. This book has already been such a blessing in my life, and I know it will be a blessing to anyone who reads it. Apostle Fred saw something in me and had faith in my gift before I could even see it myself. He asked me if I could paint for his new book, and I hesitated to say yes. If I have learned anything from my walk with the Lord, it is to say yes when a man of God sees something fit for you to do. While painting each painting, I would ask the Lord to guide me as I listened to worship music and did something I was passionate about. I felt so honored and just couldn't believe the love and support I got after showing everyone each painting. These paintings have helped me be able to receive donations towards my mission trip to Haiti with Cornerstone Covenant World Missions. The Lord has provided in such a way that I am speechless. As each person receives a painting, they tell me a vision or how the painting has touched their heart. The Lord is so good, and I am so thankful he has given me the gift of painting.

I pray I can someday reach people around the world through my paintings to help bring them closer to the Lord. Thank you, Apostle Fred, for believing in me and being such a blessing in my life. I am so thankful the Lord put me at Cornerstone Covenant Church.

Sasha Beach

Cornerstone Covenant Church, Hudson, NC

There are few men today that carry themselves like my dear friend Apostle Fred Stapleton. He has such insight into the Scriptures and understanding of God's Word and this book is another prime example of his love and dedication to living a life of teaching so that others might find themselves even closer to understanding just who Jesus is and who we are in Him. Thank you for all you do for the Kingdom and for allowing us to take this journey with you in this wonderful book.

Evangelist Barry E. Greer

Remnant Harvest Ministries, Lenoir, NC

Apostle Fred Stapleton has done it again in his 2nd book, *Journey Through the Feasts of the Lord.* A truly remarkable dive into the Feasts of the Lord and their spiritual meaning for all mankind. This is a great tool for knowledge and growth into knowing the life of Jesus Christ!

Pastor Tim Stilwell

Co-Vice President of Cornerstone Covenant World Missions

Full Gospel Sunrise Church, Connelly Springs, NC

DEDICATION

Though there are many Christian people who have influenced my values in my life, I believe there is one person who showed me a lot more than the rest—a lovely lady who is my Mom (Mary Fleenor). My mom taught me to work and strive with all my heart to do whatever it is that Jesus wants me to do. She also taught me it comes with a price. She has shown me that if I want to succeed in the Lord, then I will have to pray! I will have to give it my all.

Another important value that she taught me is if I am going to start something, then I have to complete it. This value has played a big part in my ministry and the call of God in my life. It is what motivated me to continue to do missions even though I have many challenges with my health! When my natural father had forsaken us, my mom never forsook us. She took the responsibility of raising her children seriously and worked diligently to take care of us. At times, she would tell us to eat first because she knew she didn't have enough food. My beloved Mom taught me to pray and love Jesus with all my heart. She taught me how to love people even if they did me wrong. I am very thankful for her, my lovely precious sweet Mom!

TABLE OF CONTENTS

PREFACE

In a time when biblical truth should appear on the "Most Wanted List" of every born-again believer, it is quickly being replaced by social agendas and religious ideologies. Many have found themselves in the same place that the Church of Ephesus found themselves. They had left their First Love. Revelation 2:5a gives us clear direction on how to return to our rightful place in the Kingdom of God—*"Remember therefore from whence thou art fallen, and repent."*

In his latest book, *Journey Through the Feasts of the Lord*, Apostle Fred Stapleton will explore the rich and profound meaning behind the feasts, and how each one points to the ultimate fulfillment in Jesus Christ. By using the greatest historical manuscript ever written, The Bible, he brings a clear understanding for the spiritual significance of each feast for the believers today as well as giving a roadmap that leads us back to our First Love, biblical truth.

The Feasts of the Lord are sacred and significant times for the believers to come together and celebrate the goodness and faithfulness of God. Throughout the Bible, we see various feasts that were established by God as a way for His people to remember His deliverance, provision, and promises. As you delve into *Journey Through the Feasts of the Lord*, may your heart be stirred with gratitude for the redemptive work of Christ and the hope we have in Him. May this book serve as a guide to deepen your understanding of each feast and to draw closer to the Lord as you celebrate His goodness and faithfulness.

I have had the privilege of knowing and serving alongside of Apostle Fred Stapleton for close to thirty years. I have found him to be a man of integrity. His love and compassion for the people of the world is seen in his heart for missions. Apostle Stapleton is highly respected across the United States and around the world. It is a privilege to not only know Apostle Fred Stapleton as a co-laborer in the Kingdom of God, but I am also honored to call him friend.

I strongly recommend this powerful and on-time word concerning the *Journey Through the Feasts of the Lord.*

Bishop W. Anthony Hudgins, D. Min.

ACKNOWLEDGEMENTS

Connie and I would like to express our deepest appreciation to our spiritual parents, the late David Eugene and Goldine Stines, for teaching me about the Feasts of the Lord. Much of my understanding of the feasts came from sitting under such a great man and woman of God.

Our heartfelt thanks goes out to the wonderful congregation of Cornerstone Covenant Church for all of your years of love and support.

Our deepest appreciation goes to Cornerstone Covenant World Missions, the Board Members, and Ambassadors for your love and support. Also, to all of our many ministerial friends all over the world, with special recognition to Pastor Neal Hendrix and Pastor Ken Souder, my dearest friends.

A special thank you to our daughter, Joy Danielle Boyd, for her commitment and hard work in helping us publish this book. She has done a wonderful job, and we are truly grateful.

To our other daughters, Hannah Hatch, Priscilla Shell, and Rebekah Soots, we would like to thank them for their love and support.

To Sasha Beach, we would like to thank her for the beautiful artwork she custom designed for this book. Each picture was created by her. She did an amazing job! We want to dedicate this book to our beautiful grandchildren, Parker, Braxton, Aliyah, Brooklyn, Kolton, Dezlyn, Journey, Ethan, Carson, Greyson, Hannah, and Ben. They are a great joy to us and gifts from the Lord that we will cherish forever. We pray they carry our ministry legacy on to the nations.

INTRODUCTION

First, I would like to thank you for choosing this book, *Journey Through the Feasts of the Lord.* My heart's desire is that as you read and study this book, you will get a greater understanding of what Jesus did for you in the Feasts of the Lord and what He is still doing for you in His resurrection. My prayer is that you will surely discover hidden treasures of His truth.

Surely there is a vein (a mine) for the silver, and a place for gold where they fine it." Job 28:1

Silver and gold are not found on the surface of the earth. You must dig for them. I have been digging for all the truth and a greater understanding of the Word of God for over fifty years now.

Proverbs 25:2—"*It is the glory of God to conceal a thing: but the honour of kings is to search out a matter.*" God's glory is concealed in His Word, but the honor of kings is to dig and search out those treasures hidden in Scripture. We will dig out many treasures in this book hidden under the surface.

We have looked over a vast treasure of **truth** concerning the Feasts of the Lord. Get your notebook and pen and let's go on a treasure hunt together. You will uncover treasures beyond what I will share with you. We love you.

Look with me in Proverbs 15:15-17—"*All the days of the afflicted are evil: but he that is of a* ***merry heart*** *hath a continual feast. Better is little with the fear of the LORD than great treasure and trouble therewith. Better is a dinner of herbs where love is, than a stalled ox and hatred therewith.*"

When I started writing this, we were in the Days of Awe (repentance). It starts with the Feast of Trumpets which is the first day of the seventh month. Then the Days of Awe go on for ten days, ending with the Day of Atonement.

This is a time to make amends with those you have wronged. During the Days of Awe, Jews are taught the three pillars of life. No one pillar stands alone; you need all three.

These three pillars are:

- Torah (the Word of God)
- Prayer
- Being Compassionate through Giving

The three pillars are taught in the Scriptures as **the Way, the Truth, and the Life—the Father, the Son, and the Holy Spirit—Righteousness, Peace, and Joy—Abraham, Isaac, and Jacob.**

1 John 5:7-8—*"For there are three that bear record in heaven, the Father, the Word, and the Holy Ghost: and these three are one. And there are three that bear witness in earth, the Spirit, and the water, and the blood: and these three agree in one."*

Jesus in the Seven Feasts of the Lord

Bible Study The Feasts of Israel

Leviticus 23 briefly covers all the Feasts of the Lord. There are three annual feasts that the Lord commanded all of Israel to celebrate in Jerusalem: Pesach (Passover), Shavuot (Pentecost), and Sukkot (Feast of Tabernacles). Each of these feasts, regardless of when or how it is celebrated, is called the same thing: a "Holy Convocation." (a Holy Convocation is a sacred assembly of Israel that God commanded to be held on special feast days.)

In the book of Isaiah, chapter 1, we are told God hated **their feasts or appointed times**. Also, in the book of John, chapter 7, they **call it the feast of the Jews**. Why did He hate their feasts? Because they were no longer the Lord's feasts but had become man's feasts. Jesus fulfilled all four of these Feasts of Passover which consist of Passover, Unleavened Bread, First Fruits, and Pentecost. Jesus didn't do away with them, but they became continuous feasts. We can partake of them anytime or any season if our hearts are after the Lord.

CHAPTER 1

GOD INSTITUTES THE FEAST OF PASSOVER

Before you begin this study on Passover, we suggest you read all of Exodus 12. Passover is three in one. It consists of the Feast of Passover, the Feast of Unleavened Bread, and the Feast of Firstfruits. Passover in Hebrew (*Pesach*) means "a passing over" or "to hover over." In Greek, "*Pascha*" is derived from the Hebrew "Passover."

Exodus 12:27—*"That ye shall say, It is the sacrifice of the LORD's passover, who passed over the houses of the children of Israel in Egypt, when he smote the Egyptians, and delivered our houses. And the people bowed the head and worshipped."*

Hebrews 11:28—*"Through faith he kept the passover, and the sprinkling of blood, lest he that destroyed the firstborn should touch them."* Two thoughts are involved in this word. The thought of passing in judgment of the death angel, but also the thought of hovering over in divine protection.

Mercy and judgment are linked together in this feast, as we will see as we go along.

Exodus 12:1—*"And the LORD spake unto Moses and Aaron in the land of Egypt, saying,.."* Remember, as you study, these are the words of the Lord, not Moses or Aaron's words.

Exodus 12:2—*"This month shall be unto you the beginning of months: it shall be the first month of the year to you."* The beginning of the month! Your new beginning! The fact it took place in the first month showed that God has more in mind for them in the months ahead.

Exodus 12:3—*"Speak ye unto all the congregation of Israel, saying, In the tenth day of this month they shall take to them every man a lamb, according to the house of their fathers, a lamb for an house:"*

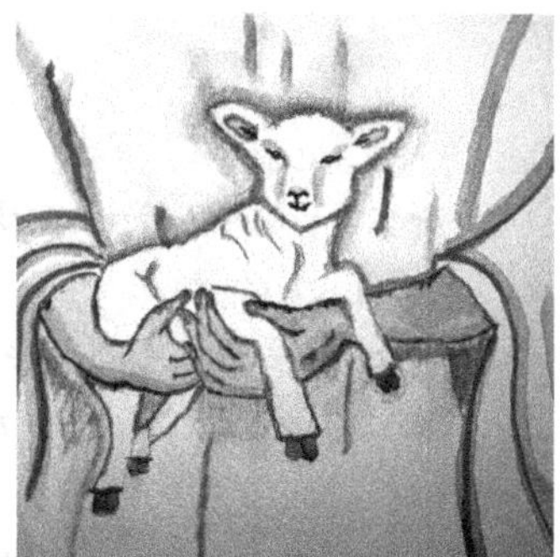

On the 10th day of the month, they would take a **lamb** for each house. They would bring the **lamb** into the house for four days. The family would fall in love with the **lamb**. One of the children may have said, "**Abba**, why do we have a **lamb** in the house?"

The father probably said, "God is going to bring judgment, and this **lamb** is going to give His life to save us. Be thankful for the Lamb; God's judgment will surely come." Then the father would point to the lamb and say, "This spotless, perfect, without blemish **lamb** is going to die, and his blood is going to save us." The day Jesus came into Jerusalem was the 10th day of Abib (Nisan). He was crucified on the 14th day.

Jesus came after 4,000 years. One day to the Lord is like a thousand years! 2 Peter 3:8-9—*"But, beloved, be not ignorant of this one thing, that one day is with the Lord as a thousand years, and a thousand years as one day. The Lord is not slack concerning his promise, as some men count slackness; but is longsuffering to us-ward, not willing that any should perish, but that all should come to repentance."*

Jesus was slain before the foundation of the world. 1 Peter 1:18-21—*"Forasmuch as ye know that ye were not redeemed with corruptible things, as silver and gold, from your vain conversation received by tradition from your fathers; But with the precious blood of Christ, as of a lamb without blemish and without spot: Who verily was foreordained before the foundation of the world, but was manifest in these last times for you, Who by him do believe in God, that raised him up from the dead, and gave him glory; that your faith and hope might be in God."*

Revelation 13:8—*"And all that dwell upon the earth shall worship him, whose names are not written in the book of life of the Lamb slain from the foundation of the world."*

A lamb for a house in Exodus 12:3-4—*"Speak ye unto all the congregation of Israel, saying, In the tenth day of this month they shall take to them every man a lamb, according to the house of their fathers, a lamb for an house: And if the household be too little for the lamb, let him and his neighbour next unto his house take it according to the number of the souls; every man according to his eating shall make your count for the lamb."*

Exodus 12:34—*"And the people took their dough before it was leavened, their kneading-troughs being bound up in their clothes upon their shoulders."*

A lamb for a nation in Exodus 29:38-42—*"Now this is that which thou shalt offer upon the altar; two lambs of the first year day by day continually.*

The one lamb thou shalt offer in the morning; and the other lamb thou shalt offer at even: And with the one lamb a tenth deal of flour mingled with the fourth part of an hin of beaten oil; and the fourth part of an hin of wine for a drink offering. And the other lamb thou shalt offer at even, and shalt do thereto according to the meat offering of the morning, and according to the drink offering thereof, for a sweet savour, an offering made by fire unto the LORD. This shall be a continual burnt offering throughout your generations at the door of the tabernacle of the congregation before the LORD: where I will meet you, to speak there unto thee."

A lamb for the world in John 1:29—"*The next day John seeth Jesus coming unto him, and saith, Behold the Lamb of God, which taketh away the sin of the world.*"

John 1:36—"*And looking upon Jesus as he walked, he saith,* ***Behold the Lamb of God!***"

Exodus 12:5-6—"*Your lamb shall be without blemish, a male of the first year: ye shall take it out from the sheep, or from the goats: And ye shall keep it up until the fourteenth day of the same month: and the whole assembly of the congregation of Israel shall kill it in the evening.*" A **lamb** that was firstborn.

The theme of the firstborn runs throughout all of Scripture: Cain is set aside for Abel, Ishmael is set aside for Isaac, Esau is set aside for Jacob, and the first Adam is set aside for the last Adam.

Our first birth is when we are born of the flesh, and it is set aside for our second birth, which is our **spiritual birth** (being born again). The first birth constitutes us as sinners because we were born in sin; the second constitutes us as the righteousness of God.

The **lamb** must be inspected. John 1:29—"*The next day John seeth Jesus coming unto him, and saith, Behold the Lamb of God, which taketh away the sin of the world.*"

Notice in this verse that it says sin, not sins. Jewish law required four days for the chief priest to inspect the **Passover lamb.** The **lamb** was thoroughly inspected for blemishes or anything that would disqualify it from being an acceptable sacrifice. Afterwards, if there were no spots or blemishes found, the high priest would declare, "**BEHOLD THE LAMB**, I find no fault in Him." Jesus arrived in Jerusalem on the tenth day of the month. On four separate occasions, He was inspected by the chief priest, rulers of the temple, and secular authorities. They all came to the same conclusion: "I find no fault in Him."

I advise you to please go read the scriptures on each one:

- **Pilate** (John 18:28-38 and John 19:4-6)
- **Herod** (Luke 23:7-18)
- **Annas and Caiaphas** (John 18:12-28)
- **Judas** (Matthew 27:3-10)
- **Centurion** (Matthew 27:54)
- **Repentant Thief** (Luke 23:39-43)

Notice: The **lamb** is inspected, not the members of the house. They did not check who was worthy inside the house. The angel only checked for the **blood of the lamb** on the doorposts and the lintel. None of us is worthy; only the **precious blood of Jesus** can cover us.

Revelation 5:12—"*Saying with a loud voice, Worthy is the Lamb that was slain to receive power, and riches, and wisdom, and strength, and honour, and glory, and blessing.*"

The **lamb** must be offered up by faith. Hebrews 11:28—"*Through faith he kept the passover, and the sprinkling of blood, lest he that destroyed the firstborn should touch them.*"

Exodus 12:7—"*And they shall take of the blood, and strike it on the two side posts and on the upper door post of the houses, wherein they shall eat it.*"

Exodus 12:13—"*And the blood shall be to you for a token upon the houses where ye are: and when I see the blood, I will pass over you, and the plague shall not be upon you to destroy you, when I smite the land of Egypt.*"

Exodus 12:22—"*And ye shall take a bunch of hyssop, and dip it in the blood that is in the bason, and strike the lintel and the two side posts with the blood that is in the bason; and none of you shall go out at the door of his house until the morning.*" The blood must be shed in the basin and applied with hyssop (humility) to the door. In those days, when people dedicated their houses to the **Lord**, they did so by making a sacrifice at the threshold of their home. In verse 22, they dipped the hyssop in the blood in the basin and then applied the blood to both sides and the lintel of the door. They were careful to step, leap, and jump over the blood. To trample underfoot the blood was to show contempt and rejection of the covenant. They believe that God stood at the door, protecting them. The common belief is that God somehow passed by their houses where the blood was applied, but it is much more, because when they applied the blood, they were inviting their God to stand in the doorway. The **lamb** was slain at the door, and the blood was drained into the basin (a ditch was dug in the door to keep the water out).

Exodus 12:22-23—*"And ye shall take a bunch of hyssop, and dip it in the blood that is in the bason, and strike the lintel and the two side posts with the blood that is in the bason; and none of you shall go out at the door of his house until the morning. For the Lord will pass through to smite the Egyptians; and when he seeth the blood upon the lintel, and on the two side posts, the LORD will pass over the door, and will not suffer the destroyer to come in unto your houses to smite you."*

Psalms 51:7—*"Purge me with hyssop, and I shall be clean: wash me, and I shall be whiter than snow."* Hyssop also means "forgiveness."

The word **Passover** means to "hover," not to just pass by. When the angel looked at the door, he saw the blood of the lamb. The blood was in the basin, and no one was allowed to step on it. We are not supposed to trample on the blood of Jesus. The blood on the doorpost was a picture of the **lamb.** Jesus was hovering over the earth. The doorpost was a symbol of the cross; that is why the Lord said, "If I be lifted up from the earth, I will draw all men unto me." Jesus was the one hovering at the door. Jesus said, "**I am the door**." Jesus' blood was poured out on the earth (basin). It was not enough that the blood of the **lamb** was poured out. It must be applied. Only when it was applied was the condemnation of death removed. When applied, it was a **sign of a covenant**. It formed the Hebrew letter "**Chet**."

Here are some interesting facts about "Chet":

- Chet means "light," and Jesus is the light of the world.
- Chet is the 8th letter of the Hebrew alphabet.
- The number eight (8) means "New Beginning" in numeric value.
- Chet is also the letter for **life**, the letter for **grace**, and the letter for **wisdom**.

Importance of the number eight (8):

- The covenant of circumcision occurs on the eighth (8th) day of a boy's life.
- There were eight souls saved in the Ark because Noah found grace in God's sight (Noahic Covenant).
- The Lord reaffirmed His covenant with Abraham eight times.
- David was the 8th son of Jesse.
- God established the Davidic Covenant with David.

Each new beginning starts with a fresh covenant. Chet is formed from the letters Vav and Zayin. They are connected by what is called a yoke. A yoke is a connection between two things that move and work together. Vav is the 6th letter of the Hebrew alphabet and means "hook." It also means "light from God to man." Zayin is the 7th letter of the Hebrew alphabet and is considered a symbol of a "crown (a king scepter), weapon-Sword of the Spirit (WORD)", and also bread (sustain) (bread of life). The letter itself resembles a sword with a handle and a staff.

Notice: They were to strike the blood of the **lamb** on the doorposts and lintel. Jesus was beaten thirty-nine times. The law for beating was thirteen times on the left side and thirteen times on the right side (the doorposts), then thirteen times on the chest (the lintel).

Exodus 12:8-10—*"And they shall eat the flesh in that night, roast with fire, and unleavened bread; and with bitter herbs they shall eat it. Eat not of it raw, nor sodden at all with water, but roast with fire; his head with his legs, and with the purtenance thereof. And ye shall let nothing of it remain until the morning; and that which remaineth of it until the morning ye shall burn with fire."* They were commanded to eat the flesh of the **lamb**. The flesh represented the Body of Jesus.

Hebrews 10:19-21—*"Having therefore, brethren, boldness to enter into the holiest by the blood of Jesus, By a new and living way, which he hath consecrated for us, through the veil, that is to say, his flesh; And having an high priest over the house of God;"*

The **lamb** cannot be eaten raw or sodden. It must go through the fire. It could not be sodden with water (the Gospel of Jesus is not to be watered down). The **fire** is God's judgment that falls on the **lamb**, not the members of the household. God took our sins and placed them on Jesus. Eat only unleavened bread (pure bread). Leaven represented sin. This is why Jesus was the only one without sin who could have been the Passover Lamb. All our sins were placed on Him.

Eat bitter herbs to remind them of their Egyptian bondage, which made their lives bitter. Sometimes we need to be reminded of where the Lord brought us from. Calvary was a bitter experience for Jesus. Eat all the **lamb** whole: head **(His mind)**, legs **(His walk)**, pertinence **(His heart)**, liver, intestines, etc., which means inward motives and affections of Christ. All three of these represented the **righteousness of God**. We must all be partakers of the Lamb **(we must eat of the righteousness of God)**.

Romans 14:17—*"For the kingdom of God is not meat and drink; but righteousness, and peace, and joy in the Holy Ghost."*

Exodus 12:11—*"And thus shall ye eat it; with your loins girded, your shoes on your feet, and your staff in your hand; and ye shall eat it in haste: it is the LORD's passover."* It was not to be eaten in a casual manner.

1. The loins were to be girded, which means "to be ready to work or go." Normally, they ate without their loins girded. 1 Peter 1:13—*"Wherefore gird up the loins of your mind, be sober, and hope to the end for the grace that is to be brought unto you at the revelation of Jesus Christ;"*

2. Your shoes on your feet. Ephesians 6:13—*"Wherefore take unto you the whole armour of God, that ye may be able to withstand in the evil day, and having done all, to stand."* The Jews, as in many other cultures, did not wear shoes while in their house. They only put shoes on when they were ready to go outside, but here they are being told to wear them in their house.

Your staff is in your hands. The lamb must be eaten in haste. Hebrews 11:13—*"These all died in faith, not having received the promises, but having seen them afar off, and were persuaded of them, and embraced them, and confessed that they were strangers and pilgrims on the earth."* The purpose of how you were dressed and eating with haste was to be prepared at a moment's notice to be ready to battle.

Acts 12:3-8—*"And because he saw it pleased the Jews, he proceeded further to take Peter also. (Then were the days of unleavened bread.) And when he had apprehended him, he put him in prison, and delivered him to four quaternions of soldiers to keep him; intending after Easter to bring him forth to the people. Peter therefore was kept in prison: but prayer was made without ceasing of the church unto God for him. And when Herod would have brought him forth, the same night Peter was sleeping between two soldiers, bound with two chains: and the keepers before the door kept the prison. And, behold, the angel of the Lord came upon him, and a light shined in the prison: and he smote Peter on the side, and raised him up, saying, Arise up quickly. And his chains fell off from his hands. And the angel said unto him, Gird thyself, and bind on thy sandals. And so he did. And he saith unto him, Cast thy garment about thee, and follow me."*

The angel told Peter to put on his sandals and to gird himself because he was about to take a journey.

Not long after the blood has been applied to your heart, you must begin to put on the Lord Jesus Christ and eat of His Word, because you are getting ready to be thrust into a battle. He brought them out as armies.

Exodus 12:51—*"And it came to pass the selfsame day, that the Lord did bring the children of Israel out of the land of Egypt by their armies."*

Exodus 12:15—*"Seven days shall ye eat unleavened bread; even the first day ye shall put away leaven out of your houses: for whosoever eateth leavened bread from the first day until the seventh day, that soul shall be cut off from Israel."*

Exodus 12:19—*"Seven days shall there be no leaven found in your houses: for whosoever eateth that which is leavened, even that soul shall be cut off from the congregation of Israel, whether he be a stranger, or born in the land."*

Exodus 12:20—*"Ye shall eat nothing leavened; in all your habitations shall ye eat unleavened bread."*

All leaven must be put away. It was a time of great cleansing. It is where we get our saying of "spring-cleaning." Leaven is a bit of sour dough (leaven puffs up). It works silently, secretly, and gradually, until the whole is leavened. Galatians 5:9—*"A little leaven leaveneth the whole lump."* Leaven (spiritually) represents sin.

Leaven of Herod (Mark 8:15): Herod was very sinful, but he feared the word of God in John's mouth. He was not willing to repent (the spirit of worldliness).

Leaven of the Sadducees (Matthew 3:7, Matthew 16:6, Matthew 16:12, Mark 12:8, Acts 5:17, Acts 23:6-8): It was their doctrine. They did not believe in the supernatural, in the spiritual, in angels, or in the resurrection of the body after death.

Leaven of the Pharisees (Luke 12:1) and Hypocrisy (Luke 11:37-44): They say and do not. They do not practice what they preach. The Pharisees were religious; they fasted, prayed, tithed, and believed in the supernatural and in Scripture. On the outside, they were clean, but inside, they were unclean and rotten to the bone!

Leaven of the Corinthian Church (1 Corinthians 5:1-13, 2 Corinthians 12:20-21): Pride means to puff up. Their sin was unchecked. This sin and other sins that are not dealt with affect others.

Leaven of Galatia and Legalism (Galatians 5:9).

"And the LORD said unto Moses and Aaron, This is the ordinance of the passover: There shall no stranger eat thereof: But every man's servant that is bought for money, when thou hast circumcised him, then shall he eat thereof. A foreigner and an hired servant shall not eat thereof. In one house shall it be eaten; thou shalt not carry forth ought of the flesh abroad out of the house; neither shall ye break a bone thereof. All the congregation of Israel shall keep it. And when a stranger shall sojourn with thee, and will keep the passover to the LORD, let all his males be circumcised, and then let him come near and keep it; and he shall be as one that is born in the land: for no uncircumcised person shall eat thereof. One law shall be to him that is homeborn, and unto the stranger that sojourneth among you. Thus did all the children of Israel; as the LORD commanded Moses and Aaron, so did they. And it came to pass the selfsame day, that the LORD did bring the children of Israel out of the land of Egypt by their armies."
(Exodus 12:43-51)

A stranger, foreigner, or hired servant was not allowed to eat unless he was circumcised. Circumcision was a sign of covenant. If they were not in a covenant relationship with the LORD, then they were not entitled to the promise and blessings of Abraham. True circumcision is of the **heart** and not of the flesh!

The **feast** is to be kept in sincerity and truth!

1 Corinthians 5:7-8—*"Purge out therefore the old leaven, that ye may be a new lump, as ye are unleavened. For even Christ our passover is sacrificed for us: Therefore let us keep the feast, not with old leaven, neither with the leaven of malice and wickedness; but with the unleavened bread of sincerity and truth."*

2 Corinthians 5:21—*"For he hath made him to be sin for us, who knew no sin; that we might be made the righteousness of God in him."*

The best illustration I have used of this scripture is the following thought:

Imagine you're standing before God as a checking account, and your sins are debts. Your debts are so many that you're overdrawn. It is so over-drawn that it is impossible for you to pay.

So, you are made a slave to your debtors. Jesus comes and pays it in full. You are now free from your debtors. How much is your account now? It is zero; that is better than negative, but it is still zero. The exciting thing is that Jesus makes a deposit in your account. He deposits **His righteousness**, which is the character of Jesus that will perfect you. He replaces your self-righteousness, which got you in debt in the first place, with **His righteousness**. I want to ask you: how much is in your account now? I say unto you, it is infinite (cannot be counted).

CHAPTER 2

PASSOVER OR EASTER?

The history of the church will tell you that the early church had no connection to Easter whatsoever. Easter replaced Passover in the second century. The Passover has been kept since the night God brought the Israelites out of Egypt. Easter has been held since Babylon. Both were celebrated before Christ. Jesus Christ was the Passover lamb, not the Easter bunny.

Both were celebrated close together. Passover is a command from God, and Easter is a pagan feast. If you will notice, none of the Feasts of the Lord were commercialized and mixed with non-Jewish or non-Christian traditions like the Easter bunny and hunting for Easter eggs (which can be traced back to practices established by Semiramis). Rabbits have long been associated with fertility and their goddess, Ishtar. Ancient Babylonians believed in a fable about an egg that fell into the Euphrates River from heaven, from which Queen Astarte (another name for Ishtar or Semiramis) was hatched. The early church would have no part of such a feast, and we wonder why they had power with God that is lacking in the modern church. Now, let's look at Acts 12.

Coming to the word "Easter," in Acts 12:4—*"And when he had apprehended him, he put him in prison, and delivered him to four quaternions of soldiers to keep him; intending after Easter to bring him forth to the people."* Some say they have found no proof that the Bible is not perfect. I beg to differ with them. Easter, as we know, if we are students of the Bible, comes from the ancient pagan festival of Astarte, also known as Ishtar.

This festival was always held in late April, after Passover. In its original form, it was a celebration of the earth "regenerating" itself after the winter season. This festival (Easter) involved a celebration of reproduction. That is why the symbol of Easter is the rabbit (the same as *Playboy* magazine) and the egg. Both are known for their reproduction. The center of attention for the festival was the female deity "Astarte." She is known in Scripture as the "queen of heaven." Jeremiah 7:18—*"The children gather wood, and the fathers kindle the fire, and the women knead their dough, to make cakes to the queen of heaven, and to pour out drink offerings unto other gods, that they may provoke me to anger."*

Jeremiah 44:17-25—"*But we will certainly do whatsoever thing goeth forth out of our own mouth, to burn incense unto the queen of heaven, and to pour out drink offerings unto her, as we have done, we, and our fathers, our kings, and our princes, in the cities of Judah, and in the streets of Jerusalem: for then had we plenty of victuals, and were well, and saw no evil. But since we left off to burn incense to the queen of heaven, and to pour out drink offerings unto her, we have wanted all things, and have been consumed by the sword and by the famine. And when we burned incense to the queen of heaven, and poured out drink offerings unto her, did we make her cakes to worship her, and pour out drink offerings unto her, without our men? Then Jeremiah said unto all the people, to the men, and to the women, and to all the people which had given him that answer, saying, The incense that ye burned in the cities of Judah, and in the streets of Jerusalem, ye, and your fathers, your kings, and your princes, and the people of the land, did not the LORD remember them, and came it not into his mind? So that the LORD could no longer bear, because of the evil of your doings, and because of the abominations which ye have committed; therefore is your land a desolation, and an astonishment, and a curse, without an inhabitant, as at this day. Because ye have burned incense, and because ye have sinned against the LORD, and have not obeyed the voice of the LORD, nor walked in his law, nor in his statutes, nor in his testimonies; therefore this evil is happened unto you, as at this day. Moreover Jeremiah said unto all the people, and to all the women, Hear the word of the LORD, all Judah that are in the land of Egypt: Thus saith the LORD of hosts, the God of Israel, saying; Ye and your wives have both spoken with your mouths, and fulfilled with your hand, saying, We will surely perform our vows that we have vowed, to burn incense to the queen of heaven, and to pour out drink offerings unto her: ye will surely accomplish your vows, and surely perform your vows.*"

The "queen of heaven" was the mother of Tammuz. Notice Ezekiel 8:14—"*Then he brought me to the door of the gate of the LORD's house which was toward the north; and, behold, there sat women weeping for Tammuz.*" The Corinthian Church had been involved in this practice. This is why they were practicing this sin. 1 Corinthians 5:1—"*It is reported commonly that there is fornication among you, and such fornication as is not so much as named among the Gentiles, that one should have his father's wife.*" Easter has never had any association with Jesus Christ or the Passover.

Please don't shut out what I am saying to you. I am going to reveal something amazing here! Passover was held in late March or by the middle of April, and the pagan festival of Easter was held later in the month of April. Every year, Easter is after Passover. Now, I am going to reveal a key to unlocking this mystery, the answer to why "Easter" is the right word instead of "Passover." The key to unlocking this mystery concerning "Easter," as used in verse four, is found in the Bible. The key is not found in verse 4, but in Acts 12:3—*"Then were the days of unleavened bread."* I hope you can see that. It was established when Passover took place. In Numbers 28:16-18, specifically verse 16, we see that the Passover is only on the 14th of the month of Abib. On the next day, the 15th, unleavened bread begins. Passover was first, then unleavened bread. Whenever Passover was held, it always preceded the Feast of Unleavened Bread. Passover did not happen during or after unleavened bread. The days of unleavened bread are never referred to as Passover.

Now, let's take another look at Acts 12:3-4—*"And because he saw it pleased the Jews, he proceeded further to take Peter also.* ***(Then were the days of unleavened bread.)*** *And when he had apprehended him, he put him in prison, and delivered him to four quaternions of soldiers to keep him; intending after Easter to bring him forth to the people."* Herod takes Peter during

"Unleavened Bread." Can you see that? Let's look at verse 4, where he uses the words "intending after Easter." As we have already proven, Passover happened before unleavened bread. Therefore, I believe after Easter is correct, because the pagan festival of Easter happens after Passover and Unleavened Bread, even as it does today. It wasn't a misinterpretation, but it was correct. If it was after unleavened bread, then Passover had already come and gone. Herod could not have been referring to Passover when he said Easter. He was waiting for the pagan festival of Easter, just a few days away. Herod was not a Jew but a pagan who would have worshipped the "queen of heaven." Herod had not killed Peter during the days of unleavened bread because he wanted to wait until Easter. He was going to wait until the pagan feast and make a mockery of Peter.

The Romans would kill people during a religious holiday or birthday celebration, such as John the Baptist. Matthew 14:6-11—*"But when Herod's birthday was kept, the daughter of Herodias danced before them, and pleased Herod. Whereupon he promised with an oath to give her whatsoever she would ask. And she, being before instructed of her mother, said, Give me here John Baptist's head in a charger. And the king was sorry: nevertheless for the oath's sake, and them which sat with him at meat, he commanded it to be given her. And he sent, and beheaded John in the prison. And his head was brought in a charger, and given to the damsel: and she brought it to her mother."* God led the translator of our Bible to correctly translate it as Easter. It most certainly did not refer to Passover. To change it to Passover is a mistranslation of the scripture.

Next, we will look at Peter being released by the angel during Unleavened Bread! Let's look at Peter in prison in Acts 12:6—*"And when Herod would have brought him forth, the same night Peter was sleeping between two soldiers, bound with two chains: and the keepers before the door kept the prison."* It was like the Lord waiting until just before Peter was to be brought before Herod for sentencing. Again, look at Acts 12:1-9.

This all happened during Unleavened Bread. I suggest that the angel released Peter just as Unleavened Bread was coming to an end because Herod would sentence him the following day. The angel delivered Peter from Herod, just like they were delivered from Pharoah's hand.

Acts 12:5—*"Peter was therefore kept in prison: but prayer was made without ceasing of the church unto God for him."* The church prayed for Peter. They were constant in prayer (constant means earnest). The same Greek word (ektenos) is used for the agonizing prayer of Jesus in the Garden of Gethsemane.

They prayed to God. They have a consciousness of coming before His presence. Many times, we pray without even being conscious of His presence. That night, Peter was sleeping, showing no signs of anxiety, because he was still young. He believed what Jesus said to him in John 21:18—*"Verily, verily, I say unto thee, When thou wast young, thou girdest thyself, and walkedst whither thou wouldest: but when thou shalt be old, thou shalt stretch forth thy hands, and another shall gird thee, and carry thee whither thou wouldest not."* He was not yet old.

Now, let's go to Acts 12:21—*"And upon a set day Herod, arrayed in royal apparel, sat upon his throne, and made an oration to them."* What does it mean by "set day"? A time set beforehand, an appointed public day. I would suggest to you that this is Easter, spoken of in Acts 12:4—*"And when he had apprehended him, he put him in prison, and delivered him to four quaternions of soldiers to keep him; intending after Easter to bring him forth to the people."* This is the day Herod was waiting for. Herod exalted himself and sought the praise of men. Early in Acts 12, it says that *"he killed James the brother of John with the sword. And because he saw it pleased the Jews."* He then took Peter; in other words, what drove Herod was his desire to be popular. He loved power, and he loved the praise of men. James and Peter taught you to deny yourself. There was no way Herod was going to do that. Just like Herod Antipas (tetrarch) took offense at John the Baptist. Luke 3:1—*"Now in the fifteenth year of the reign of Tiberius Caesar, Pontius Pilate being governor of Judaea, and Herod being tetrarch of Galilee, and his brother Philip tetrarch of Ituraea and of the region of Trachonitis, and Lysanias the tetrarch of Abilene,"* Luke 3:19—*"But Herod the tetrarch, being reproved by him for Herodias his brother Philip's wife, and for all the evils which Herod had done,"* had him killed to please others. This is exactly what Herod was seeking, and it shows on this set day. Herod was angry with Tyre and Sidon.

Acts 12:20—*"And Herod was highly displeased with them of Tyre and Sidon: but they came with one accord to him, and, having made Blastus the king's chamberlain their friend, desired peace; because their country was nourished by the king's country."*

They needed nourishment or food from the king's supply. So, somehow, they came to please Herod, which is exactly what Herod wanted. Peter was not going to give Herod what he wanted! Peter sought to please the Lord. Herod was pleased by having himself exalted, but the apostles were pleased by having Jesus Christ exalted. To Herod, if it took killing Christians to be exalted, then he would do that. On that set day (appointed day), Herod put on his royal robes, sat on the throne, and made an oration (speech) to the people. He wanted everybody to see how great he was. He was God to himself, and because he had control over the food supply, he was god over the people. Jesus and the apostles did not teach this.

Luke 22:25-26—*"And he said unto them, The kings of the Gentiles exercise lordship over them; and they that exercise authority upon them are called benefactors. But ye shall not be so: but he that is greatest among you, let him be as the younger; and he that is chief, as he that doth serve."* King Herod was exalting himself, saying, "You are dependent on me," but not so in God's Kingdom. The leader serves in the Kingdom of God. Herod is committing treason against God!

Acts 12:22—*"And the people gave a shout, saying, It is the voice of a god, not of a man."* People commit treason with Him by shouting the voice of a god and not a man! Man can be king, president, and leader over us, but he can never be God over us. God is going to put Herod in his place.

Luke 14:11—*"For whosoever exalteth himself shall be abased; and he that humbleth himself shall be exalted."*

Luke 18:14—*"I tell you, this man went down to his house justified rather than the other: for every one that exalteth himself shall be abased; and he that humbleth himself shall be exalted."*

First, God humiliates Herod by taking his prisoner, Peter, and frustrates his desire to please the Jews. God sent His angel to show Herod that not even four squads of soldiers could hold him.

Chains fell off Peter; the iron gate couldn't hold him. Acts 12:11 sums it up—*"And when Peter was come to himself, he said, Now I know of a surety, that the Lord hath sent his angel, and hath delivered me out of the hand of Herod, and from all the expectation of the people of the Jews,"*

The Lord sent His angel and rescued him from Herod. You may ask, "Why did James die and not Peter?" I am not sure, but Jesus said this to James and John in Mark 10:39—*"And they said unto him, We can. And Jesus said unto them, Ye shall indeed drink of the cup that I drink of; and with the baptism that I am baptized withal shall ye be baptized:"* Some bear witness through death, others through life.

The second thing God did was humiliate Herod and take his life.

Notice: Acts 12:20-23—*"And Herod was highly displeased with them of Tyre and Sidon: but they came with one accord to him, and, having made Blastus the king's chamberlain their friend, desired peace; because their country was nourished by the king's country. And upon a set day Herod, arrayed in royal apparel, sat upon his throne, and made an oration unto them. And the people gave a shout, saying, It is the voice of a god, and not of a man. And immediately the angel of the Lord smote him, because he gave not God the glory: and he was eaten of worms, and gave up the ghost."* The angel of the Lord showed up twice. The first time to save Peter was during Unleavened Bread, and the second time to kill Herod was during Easter. The angel smote both! God then turned it all around.

"But the word of God grew and multiplied." God's Word grew and multiplied. Now, Jesus was being exalted, not Herod!
(Acts 12:24)

CHAPTER 3

RESURRECTION / FEAST OF FIRSTFRUITS

Paul stated - *"But now is Christ risen from the dead, and become the firstfruits of them that slept."* 1 Corinthians 15:20 The firstfruits are a sign that the harvest has just begun and that many more grains are yet to come. Paul is saying in 1 Corinthians that Jesus Christ was the first-fruits from among the dead (*"them that slept"*) to rise again, and that many more will yet be resurrected!

Before we begin our discussion about the empty tomb, I would like to mention the angels at the tomb. Matthew and Mark's gospels relate that one angel spoke to the woman, while Luke and John's gospels speak of two angels. Mark and Luke called the angels men, probably since angels sometimes appear in the form of men. Genesis 18:1-2—*"And the LORD appeared unto him in the plains of Mamre: and he sat in the tent door in the heat of the day; And he lift up his eyes and looked, and, lo, three men stood by him: and when he saw them, he ran to meet them from the tent door, and bowed himself toward the ground."*

Daniel 9:21—*"Yea, whiles I was speaking in prayer, even the man Gabriel, whom I had seen in the vision at the beginning, being caused to fly swiftly, touched me about the time of the evening oblation."* Matthew and Mark mentioned only one angel at the tomb, but that one angel spoke to the woman. Some say the stories contradict one another, but that is not true. In reading all four accounts, we can see that all four are right by understanding that there were two angels. However, only one of the two served as the spokesman. With this understanding, there is no reason to consider a discrepancy in the inerrant Word of God.

Let us move into John 20.

John 20:1-2—*"The first day of the week cometh Mary Magdalene early, when it was yet dark, unto the sepulchre, and seeth the stone taken away from the sepulchre. Then she runneth, and cometh to Simon Peter, and to the other disciple, whom Jesus loved, and saith unto them, They have taken away the LORD out of the sepulchre, and we know not where they have laid him."* Mary Magdalene came to the tomb of Jesus and found the stone taken away and the tomb empty. She thought someone had stolen His body. In Matthew's account, it says that when the two women went to the tomb, there was an earthquake. In Mark, it says that when the three women went to the tomb, they saw the stone rolled away. You can explain it like this: as they were approaching the tomb of Jesus, an earthquake occurred at that very moment, and the stone rolled away at their arrival.

Let me continue to put this all together for you, regarding the number of women coming to the tomb. I believe at least five women went to the tomb. Luke names three and then says other women came too. Matthew does not say that only two women were there. Mark does not say only three were there. They only focus on the women they name. John names only Mary Magdalene, but let's look at John 20:2 again—*"Then she runneth, and cometh to Simon Peter, and to the other disciple, whom Jesus loved, and saith unto them, They have taken away the LORD out of the sepulchre, and we know not where they have laid him."* When she said, *"we know not where they have laid him,"* from her statement to Peter and John, it is clear she was not alone.

John 20:3-4—*"Peter therefore went forth, and that other disciple, and came to the sepulchre. So they ran both together: and the other disciple did outrun Peter, and came first to the sepulchre."* Peter and John ran to the tomb, but John outran Peter and came to the tomb first. They ran to see for themselves. John 20:5-10—*"And he stooping down, and looking in, saw the linen clothes lying; yet went he not in. Then cometh Simon Peter following him, and went into the sepulchre, and seeth the linen clothes lie, And the napkin, that was about his head, not lying with the linen clothes, but wrapped together in a place by itself. Then went in also that other disciple, which came first to the sepulchre, and he saw, and believed. For as yet they knew not the scripture, that he must rise again from the dead. Then the disciples went away again unto their own home."* The verse says that John was *"stooping down, and looking in."*

The Greek word used for *"looking in"* is "Blepei," which means to clearly see a material. He clearly saw the grave clothes and the napkin. When they entered, they did not see the body of Jesus, but they saw the grave clothes in a certain order. Why did John say, *"wrapped together in a place by itself"*?

As you read in John 20:8-9 above, it tells us that when John saw the arrangement of the grave clothes, he believed. I am convinced, as many others are, that the grave clothes were lying exactly as the body of Jesus had lain in them. Still wrapped, no one had to lose Jesus. He just came out of the grave clothes. Linen clothes referred to the manner in which they prepared the body for burial in that day. They would wrap the linen around the entire body until they reached the neck. John saw the linen clothes lying just as they had been when the body of Jesus lay within them, but now there was no body. The wrapped linen clothes were empty. Look at the preparation of His body by Nicodemus and Joseph of Arimathea.

John 19:39-40—*"And there came also Nicodemus, which at the first came to Jesus by night, and brought a mixture of myrrh and aloes, about an hundred pound weight. Then took they the body of Jesus, and wound it in linen clothes with the spices, as the manner of the Jews is to bury."*

As they wrapped the linen clothes around the body of Jesus, they poured one hundred pounds of spices into the wrappings and upon the body of Jesus. All these liquid spices would settle and harden around the body of Jesus. When the two disciples saw this, it was inconceivable to think that someone had stolen His body out of the grave clothes bound together around Him. The two disciples saw the linen clothes lying uncut, undisturbed, just as they had been, but there was no body inside. They had to believe that the body of Jesus was miraculously removed. Look back at John 20:7—*"And the napkin, that was about his head, not lying with the linen clothes, but wrapped together in a place by itself."* The Greek word translated *"wrapped together"* actually means "twisted together."

John 20:11-12—*"But Mary stood without at the sepulchre weeping: and as she wept, she stooped down, and looked into the sepulchre, And seeth two angels in white sitting, the one at the head, and the other at the feet, where the body of Jesus had lain."*

The disciples left Mary at the tomb, or sepulchre, weeping, and as she wept, she looked in. She saw two angels, one at the head and one at the feet, where Jesus had laid. If we just read over it too quickly, we would miss it. I believe she was seeing the true Ark of the Covenant and the Mercy Seat. Remember how the Ark of the Covenant had two angels on top, one on either side?

Hebrews 9:13-14—*"For if the blood of bulls and of goats, and the ashes of an heifer sprinkling the unclean, sanctifieth to the purifying of the flesh: How much more shall the blood of Christ, who through the eternal Spirit of-*

fered himself without spot to God, purge your conscience from dead works to serve the living God?"

Romans 3:25—*"Whom God hath set forth to be a propitiation through faith in his blood, to declare his righteousness for the remission of sins that are past, through the forbearance of God;"*

1 John 2:2—*"And he is the propitiation for our sins: and not for ours only, but also for the sins of the whole world."*

1 John 4:10—*"Herein is love, not that we loved God, but that he loved us, and sent his Son to be the propitiation for our sins."*

Now read Exodus 25:17-22—*"And thou shalt make a mercy seat of pure gold: two cubits and a half shall be the length thereof, and a cubit and a half the breadth thereof. And thou shalt make two cherubims of gold, of beaten work shalt thou make them, in the two ends of the mercy seat. And make one cherub on the one end, and the other cherub on the other end: even of the mercy seat shall ye make the cherubims on the two ends thereof. And the cherubims shall stretch forth their wings on high, covering the mercy seat with their wings, and their faces shall look one to another; toward the mercy seat shall the faces of the cherubims be. And thou shalt put the mercy seat above upon the ark; and in the ark thou shalt put the testimony that I shall give thee. And there I will meet with thee, and I will commune with thee from above the mercy seat, from between the two cherubims which are upon the ark of the testimony, of all things which I will give thee in commandment unto the children of Israel."* The word "propitiation" is from the Greek word "hilasterion" and specifically means "Mercy Seat."

Hebrews 9:5—*"And over it the cherubims of glory shadowing the mercyseat; of which we cannot now speak particularly."* Most people don't realize the word "Ark" means coffin, and the linen clothes around the body of someone buried were called caskets. The Mercy Seat, when Jesus was raised, became a Throne of Grace. Hebrews 9:11-15—*"But Christ being come an high priest of good things to come, by a greater and more perfect tabernacle, not made with hands, that is to say, not of this building; Neither by the blood of goats and calves, but by his own blood he entered in once into the holy place, having obtained eternal redemption for us. For if the blood of bulls and of goats, and the ashes of an heifer sprinkling the unclean, sanctifieth to the purifying of the flesh: How much more shall the blood of Christ, who through the eternal Spirit offered himself without spot to God, purge your conscience from dead works to serve the living God? And for this cause he is the medi-*

ator of the new testament, that by means of death, for the redemption of the transgressions that were under the first testament, they which are called might receive the promise of eternal inheritance." The blood of Jesus being applied changes the Throne of Judgment into a Throne of Grace.

Hebrews 4:14-16 says—*"Seeing then that we have a great high priest, that is passed into the heavens, Jesus the Son of God, let us hold fast our profession. For we have not an high priest which cannot be touched with the feeling of our infirmities; but was in all points tempted like as we are, yet without sin. Let us therefore come boldly unto the throne of grace, that we may obtain mercy, and find grace to help in time of need."*

Exodus 25:21-22—*"And thou shalt put the mercy seat above upon the ark; and in the ark thou shalt put the testimony that I shall give thee. And there I will meet with thee, and I will commune with thee from above the mercy seat, from between the two cherubims which are upon the ark of the testimony, of all things which I will give thee in commandment unto the children of Israel."* Through the application of the blood of Jesus, the Mercy Seat becomes a place we can come to boldly and find help because it has become a place of communion. The Ark of the Covenant was a sign of the covenant. What Mary saw was the New Covenant and Jesus as the Mercy Seat.

Let's look at John 20:13-17—*"And they say unto her, Woman, why weepest thou? She saith unto them, Because they have taken away my Lord, and I know not where they have laid him. And when she had thus said, she turned herself back, and saw Jesus standing, and knew not that it was Jesus. Jesus saith unto her, Woman, why weepest thou? whom seekest thou? She, supposing him to be the gardener, saith unto him, Sir, if thou have borne him hence, tell me where thou hast laid him, and I will take him away. Jesus saith unto her, Mary. She turned herself, and saith unto him, Rabboni; which is to say, Master. Jesus saith unto her, Touch me not; for I am not yet ascended to my Father: but go to my brethren, and say unto them, I ascend unto my Father, and your Father; and to my God, and your God."* Even after seeing the angel, she still didn't understand what He had told her and thought someone had stolen His Body. One writer made the assumption that the stone had been rolled away from the grave, but not from her heart.

In verse 14, she sees Jesus but doesn't know it was Jesus. Look at John 20:15 above; she supposed Jesus to be a gardener. However, when Jesus spoke her name, "Mary," she knew Him. She turned and said to Him, "Rabboni," which means master. She approaches Him to embrace Him, and He instructs her, "No, go tell my brethren." Jesus didn't look like the Jesus she knew, but she recognized His voice. Jesus said, *"Touch me not."* She wanted to cling to Jesus, but He wanted her to go tell His brethren, as you see in verse 17. Jesus says, *"I ascend unto my Father, and your Father, and to my God, and your God."*

Jesus is saying there is a difference now because He goes to the Father. You are not coming to God as your judge, but as "Abba," "Daddy," through His blood. From disciples to brethren. Wow, what a promotion bought with the resurrection! This phrase, *"My brethren,"* speaks to the love Jesus had for them and His confidence in them to fulfill the mission He is about to give them. *"My brethren"*—Jesus told us what this title means earlier in His ministry:

Matthew 12:47-50—*"Then one said unto him, Behold, thy mother and thy brethren stand without, desiring to speak with thee. But he answered and said unto him that told him, Who is my mother? and who are my brethren? And he stretched forth his hand toward his disciples, and said, Behold my mother and my brethren! For whosoever shall do the will of my Father which is in heaven, the same is my brother, and sister, and mother."*

Romans 8:29—*"For whom he did foreknow, he also did predestinate to be conformed to the image of his Son, that he might be the firstborn among many brethren."*

John 20:19-23—*"Then the same day at evening, being the first day of the week, when the doors were shut where the disciples were assembled for fear of the Jews, came Jesus and stood in the midst, and saith unto them, Peace be unto you. And when he had so said, he shewed unto them his hands and his side. Then were the disciples glad, when they saw the LORD. Then said Jesus to them again, Peace be unto you: as my Father hath sent me, even so send I you. And when he had said this, he breathed on them, and saith unto them, Receive ye the Holy Ghost: Whose soever sins ye remit, they are remitted unto them; and whose soever sins ye retain, they are retained."*

The disciples met the resurrected Jesus. Because of their fear of the Jews, they had locked the doors. But Jesus appeared and stood in their midst. After they had forsaken Jesus at the cross and Peter denied Him, the disciples probably feared Jesus would rebuke them. John might have thought Jesus would ask, "Why aren't you watching after my mother?" They were most likely expecting some words of rebuke. But instead, He spoke a word of reconciliation to them: *"Peace be unto you."*

2 Corinthians 5:18-20—*"And all things are of God, who hath reconciled*

us to himself by Jesus Christ, and hath given to us the ministry of reconciliation; To wit, that God was in Christ, reconciling the world unto himself, not imputing their trespasses unto them; and hath committed unto us the word of reconciliation. Now then we are ambassadors for Christ, as though God did beseech you by us: we pray you in Christ's stead, be ye reconciled to God." Jesus is preparing them after this for the ministry of reconciliation.

Colossians 1:19-20—*"For it pleased the Father that in him should all fulness dwell; And, having made peace through the blood of his cross, by him to reconcile all things unto himself; by him, I say, whether they be things in earth, or things in heaven."* The blood of Jesus was shed to reconcile. It was to bring mankind back to peace with God. Adam brought death, but Jesus brought peace and life. 2 Corinthians 5:20—*"Now then we are ambassadors for Christ, as though God did beseech you by us: we pray you in Christ's stead, be ye reconciled to God."* Because of the death of Jesus, God is not counting our sins against us if we will just make the choice to accept the gift of grace, no matter what our sin is. However, we do have a part to play. We must be reconciled to God!

Ten of the disciples were present in the room where Jesus appeared, all except Thomas. It was good that the disciples stayed together. Jesus' body wasn't limited by locked doors; He miraculously stood in their midst. In Luke, he mentions this gathering and includes others with them. Luke 24:33—*"And they rose up the same hour, and returned to Jerusalem, and found the eleven gathered together, and them that were with them,"* Jesus also invited them to actually touch His body to see that it was real. Luke 24:39-40—*"Behold my hands and my feet, that it is I myself: handle me, and see; for a spirit hath not flesh and bones, as ye see me have. And when he had thus spoken, he shewed them his hands and his feet."*

Let's look back at John 20:22—*"And when he had said this, he breathed on them, and saith unto them, Receive ye the Holy Ghost:"* This very event happened on the day of Firstfruits. Does this mean they received the Holy Ghost at that time? I believe it was only a foretaste and a promise of that which the disciples would soon receive at Pentecost. It was a type of Firstfruits of the coming harvest during the Feast of Weeks, or Pentecost.

John 7:39—*"(But this spake he of the Spirit, which they that believe on him should receive: for the Holy Ghost was not yet given; because that Jesus was not yet glorified.)"* The promise was that they would receive the Holy Ghost after He ascended into heaven and became glorified. Jesus tells His disciples to tarry in Jerusalem until they are endowed with power from on high.

Luke 24:46-49—*"And said unto them, Thus it is written, and thus it behooved Christ to suffer, and to rise from the dead the third day: And that repentance and remission of sins should be preached in his name among all nations, beginning at Jerusalem. And ye are witnesses of these things. And, behold, I send the promise of my Father upon you: but tarry ye in the city of Jerusalem, until ye be endued with power from on high."*

Acts 1:4-5—*"And, being assembled together with them, commanded them that they should not depart from Jerusalem, but wait for the promise of the Father, which, saith he, ye have heard of me. For John truly baptized with water; but ye shall be baptized with the Holy Ghost not many days hence."* Acts 1:8—*"But ye shall receive power, after that the Holy Ghost is come upon you: and ye shall be witnesses unto me both in Jerusalem, and in all Judaea, and in Samaria, and unto the uttermost part of the earth."*

The act of breathing on them was a promise of what was coming. Pentecost is the fulfillment of that promise in Luke 24:49—*"And, behold, I send the promise of my Father upon you: but tarry ye in the city of Jerusalem, until ye be endued with power from on high."* The words *"until"* and *"ye shall receive"* both indicate it hadn't happened yet.

Acts 2:32-33—*"This Jesus hath God raised up, whereof we all are witnesses. Therefore being by the right hand of God exalted, and having received of the Father the promise of the Holy Ghost, he hath shed forth this, which ye now see and hear."*

Jesus was the Firstfruits of Passover, but the Day of Pentecost was the fruit of Jesus' death, burial, resurrection, ascension, and glorification, just as Jesus had promised. What the disciples received when Jesus breathed on them was a foretaste of the baptism of the Holy Ghost. Jesus breathing upon His disciples symbolized the Spirit of God. Do you remember that man was made a living soul by the breath of God? Genesis 2:7—*"And the LORD God formed man of the dust of the ground, and breathed into his nostrils the breath of life; and man became a living soul."* Jesus likened being born of the Spirit to wind or breath.

Jesus says in John 3:8—*"The wind bloweth where it listeth, and thou hearest the sound thereof, but canst not tell whence it cometh, and whither it goeth: so is every one that is born of the Spirit."* Ezekiel prophesied of the dead, dry bones being revived and restored to life by the breath of God.

Ezekiel 37:9-14—*"Then said he unto me, Prophesy unto the wind, prophesy, son of man, and say to the wind, Thus saith the Lord God; Come from the four winds, O breath, and breathe upon these slain, that they may live. So I prophesied as he commanded me, and the breath came into them, and they lived, and stood up upon their feet, an exceeding great army. Then he said unto me, Son of man, these bones are the whole house of Israel: behold, they say, Our bones are dried, and our hope is lost: we are cut off for our parts. Therefore prophesy and say unto them, Thus saith the Lord God; Behold, O my people, I will open your graves, and cause you to come up out of your graves, and bring you into the land of Israel. And ye shall know that I am the Lord, when I have opened your graves, O my people, and brought you up out of your graves, And shall put my spirit in you, and ye shall live, and I shall place you in your own land: then shall ye know that I the Lord have spoken it, and performed it, saith the Lord."*

Acts 2:2—*"And suddenly there came a sound from heaven as of a rushing mighty wind, and it filled all the house where they were sitting."* This description makes me think of the blowing of the Shofar. The Shofar makes no sound without the breath blowing through it.

Exodus 19:19—*"And when the voice of the trumpet sounded long, and waxed louder and louder, Moses spake, and God answered him by a voice."*

Then in Hebrews, referring to when Moses went to the mountain, a great fear came on the people as they heard God's voice. Hebrews 12:19—*"And the sound of a trumpet, and the voice of words; which voice they that heard intreated that the word should not be spoken to them any more:"* This wind was felt and heard.

Even as the wind, the breath, and the Spirit of God had moved upon the faces of the waters before God spoke, *"Let there be light,"* God quickened everything into life and existence with His breath and word. Genesis 1:2-3—*"And the earth was without form, and void; and darkness was upon the face of the deep. And the Spirit of God moved upon the face of the waters. And God said, Let there be light: and there was light."*

The most wonderful example of God's breath is found in Acts 2:2-4—"*And suddenly there came a sound from heaven as of a rushing mighty wind, and it filled all the house where they were sitting. And there appeared unto them cloven tongues like as of fire, and it sat upon each of them. And they were all filled with the Holy Ghost, and began to speak with other tongues, as the Spirit gave them utterance."* This was the fulfillment of the foretaste of the disciple's foretaste, as you read in John 20:22—*"And when he had said this, he breathed on them, and saith unto them, Receive ye the Holy Ghost:"* The promise became a reality on the Day of Pentecost.

Look at Acts 2:39—*"For the promise is unto you, and to your children, and to all that are afar off, even as many as the LORD our God shall call."* He told those Jews that it was unto you (Jews of that day), and your children (the whole nation of Israel), and to all that are afar off (Gentiles), as many as the Lord our God shall call. God was implying that the reality of the promise is for everyone. Jesus performed this act on ten of the eleven disciples. Thomas was not present, for whatever reason. Jesus breathed on them, but on Pentecost, He breathed in them.

The outpouring of the Holy Ghost was the Day of Pentecost being fulfilled, which until then was the Feast of Harvest. It could not happen before that day, just as Jesus could not have died on the cross a day sooner than Passover. In John 20, Jesus was not imparting the Holy Ghost to them. He was promising to do so later, at Pentecost.

John tells us that Jesus shows the disciples His scars, not once but twice. Jesus comes through the locked door and appears before the disciples, who were extremely frightened. Jesus makes it a point to show His scars to them. The other disciples tell Thomas, but Thomas doesn't believe. John 20:25—*"The other disciples therefore said unto him, We have seen the LORD. But he said unto them, Except I shall see in his hands the print of the nails, and put my finger into the print of the nails, and thrust my hand into his side, I will not believe."* Eight days later, Jesus visits the disciples again. This time, Thomas is there.

John 20:27-29—*"Then saith he to Thomas, Reach hither thy finger, and behold my hands; and reach hither thy hand, and thrust it into my side: and be not faithless, but believing. And Thomas answered and said unto him, My LORD and my God. Jesus saith unto him, Thomas, because thou hast seen me, thou hast believed: blessed are they that have not seen, and yet have believed."*

You may ask, "Why did Jesus show His wounds to His disciples after His resurrection?" Look at Acts 1:3—*"To whom also he shewed himself alive after his passion by many infallible proofs, being seen of them forty days, and speaking of the things pertaining to the kingdom of God:"* It was infallible proof that He was the same Person. Jesus said, *"Behold my hands . . . thrust it into my side."* He was identifying Himself as the same Jesus they had followed, but in a resurrected body. They had never seen Him this way before. Peter, James, and John had seen Him transfigured, His garments white as snow, but never like this. So, they were tempted to doubt Him. But when they saw His nail-printed hand and the pierced side, they believed. These marks they could not dispute. It was infallible proof.

The Greek word translated as infallible proof is "tekmerion." It refers to that which causes something or someone to be known in a convincing and decisive manner. Jesus spent time with them; He walked, talked, and even ate with them after the resurrection. These are some amazing facts that are infallible proof. The women worshipped Him and held His nailed-scarred feet.

Matthew 28:9—*"And as they went to tell his disciples, behold, Jesus met them, saying, All hail. And they came and held him by the feet, and worshipped him."* Jesus broke bread with Cleopas and an unnamed disciple. Then, after He had convinced them of the scriptures, their eyes were opened in Luke 24:30-34—*"And it came to pass, as he sat at meat with them, he took bread, and blessed it, and brake, and gave to them. And their eyes were opened, and they knew him; and he vanished out of their sight. And they said one to another, Did not our heart burn within us, while he talked with us by the way, and while he opened to us the scriptures? And they rose up the same hour, and returned to Jerusalem, and found the eleven gathered together, and them that were with them, Saying, The Lord is risen indeed, and hath appeared to Simon."*

When their eyes were opened, and they knew it was Jesus, He vanished out of their sight. They went and told the eleven disciples what happened.

Luke 24:35-36—*"And they told what things were done in the way, and how he was known of them in breaking of bread. And as they thus spake, Jesus himself stood in the midst of them, and saith unto them, Peace be unto you."* As they were telling the disciples, Jesus appeared before them.

Luke 24:37-40—*"But they were terrified and affrighted, and supposed that they had seen a spirit. And he said unto them, Why are ye troubled? and why do thoughts arise in your hearts? Behold my hands and my feet, that it is I myself: handle me, and see; for a spirit hath not flesh and bones, as ye see me have. And when he had thus spoken, he shewed them his hands and his feet."*

The rest of the story is in John 21. Jesus showed His scars as proof and then ate fish and honeycomb with them. Some didn't believe still. Luke 24:41-43—*"And while they yet believed not for joy, and wondered, he said unto them, Have ye here any meat? And they gave him a piece of a broiled fish, and of an honeycomb. And he took it and did eat before them."*

Then in Luke 24:44-49—*"And he said unto them, These are the words which I spake unto you, while I was yet with you, that all things must be fulfilled, which were written in the law of Moses, and in the prophets, and in the psalms, concerning me. Then opened he their understanding, that they might understand the scriptures, And said unto them, Thus it is written, and thus it behooved Christ to suffer, and to rise from the dead the third day: And that repentance and remission of sins should be preached in his name among all nations, beginning at Jerusalem. And ye are witnesses of these things. And, behold, I send the promise of my Father upon you: but tarry ye in the city of Jerusalem, until ye be endued with power from on high."* When He spoke this time, He opened their understanding of the scripture.

And now, finally, read with me John 20:30-31—*"And many other signs truly did Jesus in the presence of his disciples, which are not written in this book: But these are written, that ye might believe that Jesus is the Christ, the Son of God; and that believing ye might have life through his name."*

This is John's reason for writing this book, so we might believe. We might believe that Jesus is the Christ, the Anointed One, the Messiah, and the only begotten Son of God. The only way to enter life is through His name. In chapter 20, Jesus went to great lengths to equip His followers with belief and understanding of the scriptures concerning His resurrection. Their sorrow became joy.

This is a great picture of when we enter into life in the only true living way: JESUS CHRIST!

CHAPTER 4

COUNTING OF THE OMER AND THE KINGDOM

The Counting of the Omer creates a countdown from the Firstfruit (resurrection) to Shavuot (Pentecost), the time of the giving of the Torah, and the time of the giving of the Holy Spirit. Both were given at the Feast of Pentecost. Look at the encounter on the mount at Sinai. Some of the connections are obvious: The law was given to Israel fifty days after the crossing of the Red Sea, and the Spirit is given to the church fifty days after the resurrection.

There are physical signs: a great noise from heaven, whether thunder and trumpets or a mighty rushing wind, and the descent of God in fire. The gift of the law defines God's people, but the gift of the Holy Spirit refines God's people (making them a New Creation)

The people were commissioned to be a Kingdom of priests in the Old Covenant, but they rejected it and became one tribe as priests, the Levites only, and the earthly Tabernacle (Temple) is established as a pattern of what was already in heaven.

On Pentecost, the church became the **real Temple from heaven on earth.** We became a **Royal Kingdom of Priests,** not just one tribe. A sermon is preached, calling for obedience. A new covenant has started at both. The Biblical Command to Count the Omer.

The Torah writes: And you shall count for yourselves from the morrow of the Shabbat, from the day that you bring the omer [offering] that is raised, seven complete weeks there shall be until the morrow of the seventh week you shall count fifty days (Leviticus 23:15-16).

Acts have come to be called **"Acts of the Apostles,"** but originally, they were called **"Acts of Jesus Christ through His servants."** Acts 1:1—*"The former treatise have I made, O Theophilus, of all that Jesus began both to do and teach.* " The former treatise means **"word"** or **"discourse."** The word **"former"** actually means **"first"** book, which is referring to the book of Luke. It was addressed to Theophilus. Who was Theophilus? There are several different theories, but the simple fact is that we do not know who Theophilus was. The name "Theophilus" literally means "lover of God," but carries the idea of "friend of God." Some believe this is a generic title that applies to all Christians. I personally believe in both. There was an individual named Theophilus because Luke addresses him as **"the most excellent Theophilus"** in Luke's first book. Luke 1:3-4—*"It seemed good to me also, having had perfect understanding of all things from the very first, to write unto thee in order, most excellent Theophilus, That thou mightest know the certainty of those things, wherein thou hast been instructed."*

Luke, in verse 1 of Acts, is referring to his former writings in the book of Luke. At one time, the Gospel of Luke and the book of the Acts of Jesus Christ were joined together as one book with two volumes. The book of Luke is volume one, and the Acts of Jesus Christ are volume two.

Look at the phrase "all that Jesus began to do and teach." The Gospel of Luke describes only the beginning of Jesus' work on earth. Acts describes the continuation of His work on earth through His disciples **(lovers of God)** on earth. Jesus continues that work through the Holy Spirit to our present day and beyond.

Jesus is working or giving orders to His apostles from His headquarters in heaven. To make this clearer, let us look at the word **"Apostle."** During this time, the word **"Apostle"** was a naval term that described an admiral, the fleet of ships that traveled with him, and the crew that accompanied the admiral.

They would be sent out on missions to locate territories where the kingdom they represented did not exist. Once the region was identified, the admiral and his crew, along with all their car belongings, would disembark and work together to colonize the region for their king. Teaching the people of the region the language, ways, and customs of their king.

Their purpose was total colonization of the region. They would establish a new culture and a new life for the people of the new region. The apostle, or admiral, was the team leader establishing a new society. Once they completed the task, most of the team got back on the ships, went out to find another area, and repeated the entire colonization process all over again. Some were left behind as governors and leaders of the new region. The word "Apostle" describes someone who had the authority to act as "ambassador" of the king he represents to another government.

2 Corinthians 5:20-21— *"Now then we are ambassadors for Christ, as though God did beseech you by us: we pray you in Christ's stead, be ye reconciled*

to God. For he hath made him to be sin for us, who knew no sin; that we might be made the righteousness of God in him."

An apostle was an envoy sent to do business on behalf of the one who sent him.

Ephesians 6:20—*"For which I am an ambassador in bonds: that therein I may speak boldly, as I ought to speak."*

Proverbs 13:17— *"A wicked messenger falleth into mischief: but a faithful ambassador is health."*

Acts 1:2-3— *"Until the day in which he was taken up, after that he through the Holy Ghost had given commandments unto the apostles whom he had chosen: To whom also he shewed himself alive after his passion by many infallible proofs, being seen of them forty days, and speaking of the things pertaining to the kingdom of God:"*

Jesus was instructing the apostles what to do in His physical absence. Consider the phrase, **"Through the Holy Ghost had given commandments."** Jesus established the fact of His resurrection with many infallible proofs during the forty days after His resurrection but before His ascension. He left no doubt in their minds. I mentioned many infallible proofs in the last two chapters.

The apostle Paul mentions one of these many infallible proofs. 1 Corinthians 15:6—*"After that, he was seen of above five hundred brethren at once; of whom the greater part remain unto this present, but some are fallen asleep."* More than 500 people saw the resurrected Jesus, and most of them were still alive twenty-five years later, in Paul's days. Jesus used the forty days to speak to His apostles about things pertaining to the Kingdom of God. Jesus had taught them to pray. Matthew 6:10—*"Thy kingdom come, Thy will be done in earth, as it is in heaven."*

Jesus is teaching them how to establish His Kingdom on earth. The Kingdom of God is mentioned throughout the Old and New Testaments. Matthew 6:33—*"But seek ye first the kingdom of God, and his righteousness; and all these things shall be added unto you."* He tells us to seek first His Kingdom and His Righteousness.

The Lord told us to seek first His Kingdom, but in the church world today, so little is known about His Kingdom. Jesus reigns as King through Righteousness. To seek Righteousness is to seek to be under His rulership. Jesus' reign is infinite. Jesus' reign is established in God's promises, which they are waiting for in Acts 1. Here are some things Jesus would have taught them about the Kingdom of God. His Kingdom would be established on earth. Jesus mentions the Kingdom of God at the Last Supper. Mark 14:25—"*Verily I say unto you, I will drink no more of the fruit of the vine, until that day that I drink it new in the kingdom of God.*"

Let's go deeper into Matthew 6:10—"*Thy kingdom come, Thy will be done in earth, as it is in heaven.*" This is actually praying for the day when God will bring heaven to earth. God still has a plan for this planet called earth. He will rule and reign here. As believers, we will rule and reign with Him. When you are under His lordship, it is not rules and regulations but **"righteousness, peace, and joy in the Holy Ghost."** Romans 14:17—"*For the kingdom of God is not meat and drink; but righteousness, and peace, and joy in the Holy Ghost.*" The greatest prayer we can pray is for His Kingdom to come. Look at these scriptures:

Luke 11:20— "*But if I with the finger of God cast out devils, no doubt the kingdom of God is come upon you.*"

Luke 10:11— "*Even the very dust of your city, which cleaveth on us, we do wipe off against you: notwithstanding be ye sure of this, that the kingdom of God is come nigh unto you.*"

You might ask how the Kingdom is near them. The answer is that the Kingdom was near them because Jesus the King was there among them. Through the cross, Jesus inaugurated His Father's Kingdom. He used His disciples, which include us, to consummate it. Jesus is not coming as King; He already is King over heaven and earth. Matthew 28:18—"*And Jesus came and spake unto them, saying, All power is given unto me in heaven and in earth.*" It is our responsibility as the church to make the invisible Kingdom visible. The only way the Kingdom of God is manifested is by the way we, His citizens, live.

Philippians 3:20—"*For our conversation is in heaven; from whence also we look for the Saviour, the Lord Jesus Christ.*"

Acts 1:4-5—"*And, being assembled together with them, commanded them that they should not depart from Jerusalem, but wait for the promise of the Father, which, saith he, ye have heard of me. For John truly baptized with water; but ye shall be baptized with the Holy Ghost not many days hence.*" *They were all assembled together. Jesus commands them to stay in Jerusalem. His first commission was not to go, but to* **"wait."**

Luke 24:49-53—"*And, behold, I send the promise of my Father upon you: but tarry ye in the city of Jerusalem, until ye be endued with power from on high. And he led them out as far as to Bethany, and he lifted up his hands, and blessed them. And it came to pass, while he blessed them, he was parted from them, and carried up into heaven. And they worshipped him, and returned to Jerusalem with great joy: And were continually in the temple, praising and blessing God. Amen." They were to tarry (wait or stay) in Jerusalem for ten days and not depart. I have always thought they stayed in the Upper Room and did not come out.*

Acts 1:13—*"And when they were come in, they went up into an upper room, where abode both Peter, and James, and John, and Andrew, Philip, and Thomas, Bartholomew, and Matthew, James the son of Alphaeus, and Simon Zelotes, and Judas the brother of James." But it doesn't say that they stayed there; in fact, Luke 24:52-53 says—"And they worshipped him, and returned to Jerusalem with great joy: And were continually in the temple, praising and blessing God. Amen."*

They were no longer hiding but waiting before they preached the Kingdom of God to every creature.

Now we move to Acts 1:6-7—"*When they therefore were come together, they asked of him, saying, Lord, wilt thou at this time restore again the kingdom to Israel? And he said unto them, It is not for you to know the times or the seasons, which the Father hath put in his own power.*" They were still focused on the natural and not the spiritual Kingdom. I believe He will restore Israel. After over 2,000 years of not being a nation, geographical Israel became a nation again, which is also a sign of the end times.

The apostles were most likely thinking about Daniel 7:27—*"And the kingdom and dominion, and the greatness of the kingdom under the whole heaven, shall be given to the people of the saints of the most High, whose kingdom is an everlasting kingdom, and all dominions shall serve and obey him."* I want you to see something in this verse. God's everlasting Kingdom shall not be in heaven **(heaven is the throne room)** only but "under the whole heaven" too. The earth and all the dominions of man shall serve Him. The disciples were probably also thinking of God's words to Moses in Exodus 19:5-6—*"Now therefore, if ye will obey my voice indeed, and keep my covenant, then ye shall be a peculiar treasure unto me above all people: for all the earth is mine: And ye shall be unto me a kingdom of priests, and an holy nation. These are the words which thou shalt speak unto the children of Israel."*

We all need some form of government in our lives. Government has been an important concern since the first Adam, when God blessed him.

Genesis 1:28—*"And God blessed them, and God said unto them, Be fruitful, and multiply, and replenish the earth, and subdue it: and have dominion over the fish of the sea, and over the fowl of the air, and over every living thing that moveth upon the earth."* Neither Adam nor Israel had kept a covenant with God. Adam rejected God's rule, and so did Israel, because they did not want God to rule them. They wanted to rule themselves, and they lost their dominion.

1 Samuel 8:7—*"And the LORD said unto Samuel, Hearken unto the voice of the people in all that they say unto thee: for they have not rejected thee, but they have rejected me, that I should not reign over them."* Don't be harsh on Israel; America has done the same. The test of government is to whose rule you submit. There are two choices: God's or Satan's? The devil's temptations of Jesus were the same test over government in Matthew 4 and Luke 4. Pause and go read it with this in mind. Jesus' answer to the disciples' question in Acts 1:6 is found in Acts 1:7—*"It is not for you to know the times or the seasons, which the Father hath put in his own power."* Jesus was saying that even though you may be interested in this, it's not for you to know.

Jesus goes on to say in Acts 1:8—*"But ye shall receive power, after that the Holy Ghost is come upon you: and ye shall be witnesses unto me both in Jerusalem, and in all Judaea, and in Samaria, and unto the uttermost part of the earth."* The word **"power"** used in this verse is **"dunamis,"** which has the meaning of authority. The purpose of the baptism of the Holy Ghost is to receive the authority of the Holy Ghost to be witnesses. When you get saved, you receive

His Spirit, but you don't receive the authority of the Spirit until you are baptized in the Holy Ghost. Acts 1:9—*"And when he had spoken these things, while they beheld, he was taken up; and a cloud received him out of their sight."* Verse 9 indicates these are the Lord's final words before being taken.

Luke 24:46-53—*"And said unto them, Thus it is written, and thus it behooved Christ to suffer, and to rise from the dead the third day: And that repentance and remission of sins should be preached in his name among all nations, beginning at Jerusalem. And ye are witnesses of these things. And, behold, I send the promise of my Father upon you: but tarry ye in the city of Jerusalem, until ye be endued with power from on high. And he led them out as far as to Bethany, and he lifted up his hands, and blessed them. And it came to pass, while he blessed them, he was parted from them, and carried up into heaven. And they worshipped him, and returned to Jerusalem with great joy: And were continually in the temple, praising and blessing God. Amen."* Verse 53 lets us know these are words of blessing. Jesus is passing the torch. They did fulfill this next verse after Pentecost.

Some have called it the table of contents for the book of Acts. Reading through Acts, it becomes clear. The gospel is preached in Jerusalem in chapters 1-7, in Judea and Samaria in chapters 13-18, and in the uttermost parts of the earth in chapters 19-28. I must note this here: the apostles were looking for the restoration of the Kingdom in Israel. Many today say God is finished with Israel and that all His promises were transferred to the church. Jesus doesn't say He has no plans for Israel, but He refocuses their attention on His plan for them in His presence. Clearly, God is not finished with Israel. For the apostles and Luke, the ascension of Jesus was extremely important. Luke ends his first volume, the Gospel of Luke, with the Ascension, and begins with it in his second volume, Acts of Jesus Christ.

Luke 24:51-53 tells us as Jesus was carried up to heaven, they worshipped Him. They traveled back to Jerusalem with great joy. They were regularly in the temple, praising and blessing God. It was a much different reaction than when He was placed in the tomb. Their sorrow was turned into joy. They were finally realizing the benefits that would come because Jesus was going back to the Father. Their worship was a sign that they believed in the promises of Jesus.

Acts 1:11-12—*"Which also said, Ye men of Galilee, why stand ye gazing up into heaven? this same Jesus, which is taken up from you into heaven, shall so come in like manner as ye have seen him go into heaven. Then returned they unto Jerusalem from the mount called Olivet, which is from Jerusalem a sabbath day's journey."* When Jesus ascended, the payment for sin was confirmed, and the debt was paid in full! The new covenant was sealed by His blood and confirmed by His ascension.

Hebrews 10:10-14—*"By the which will we are sanctified through the offering of the body of Jesus Christ once for all. And every priest standeth daily ministering and offering oftentimes the same sacrifices, which can never take away sins: But this man, after he had offered one sacrifice for sins for ever, sat down on the right hand of God; From henceforth expecting till his enemies be made his footstool. For by one offering he hath perfected for ever them that are sanctified."* And a new covenant began. When Jesus ascended to the throne (**the Mercy Seat**), the intercessory work of Jesus on our behalf began.

1 John 2:1—*"My little children, these things write I unto you, that ye sin not. And if any man sin, we have an advocate with the Father, Jesus Christ the righteous:"*

Romans 8:34—*"Who is he that condemneth? It is Christ that died, yea rather, that is risen again, who is even at the right hand of God, who also maketh intercession for us."*

Hebrews 7:25—*"Wherefore he is able also to save them to the uttermost that come unto God by him, seeing he ever liveth to make intercession for them."*

Clearly, Jesus is actively working on our behalf even now. Jesus is interceding for us, while Satan, whose name means **"accuser,"** is accusing us day and night. He is pointing out all our sins and weaknesses to God and to us. But we have to put it under the blood. The judge, who is now our Father, declares that our debt is paid in full. 2 Corinthians 5:21—*"For he hath made him to be sin for us, who knew no sin; that we might be made the righteousness of God in him."* The disciples knew by this time what the following verse meant. 1 Timothy 2:5—*"For there is one God, and one mediator between God and men, the man Christ Jesus;"* Jesus Christ is the perfect man. He was fully man and fully God. He had to take that Body of a Man into heaven, which still exists, and send back the spiritual "man" **(Holy Spirit)** to live in us. Some today don't believe in the physical return of the Lord, but I disagree.

Acts 3:12-21—*"And when Peter saw it, he answered unto the people, Ye men of Israel, why marvel ye at this? or why look ye so earnestly on us, as though by our own power or holiness we had made this man to walk? The God of Abraham, and of Isaac, and of Jacob, the God of our fathers, hath glorified his Son Jesus; whom ye delivered up, and denied him in the presence of Pilate, when he was determined to let him go. But ye denied the Holy One and the Just, and desired a murderer to be granted unto you; And killed the Prince of life, whom God hath raised from the dead; whereof we are witnesses. And his name through faith in his name hath made this man strong, whom ye see and know: yea, the faith which is by him hath given him this perfect soundness in the presence of you all. And now, brethren, I wot that through ignorance ye did it, as did also your rulers. But those things, which God before had shewed by the mouth of all his prophets, that Christ should suffer, he hath so fulfilled. Repent ye therefore, and be converted, that your sins may be blotted out, when the times of refreshing shall come from the presence of the Lord. And he shall send Jesus Christ, which before was preached unto you: Whom the heaven must receive until the times of restitution of all things, which God hath spoken by the mouth of all his holy prophets since the world began."*

Remember what Jesus said in Luke 24:49—*"I send the promise of my Father upon you: but tarry ye in the city of Jerusalem, until ye be endued with power from on high."*

Acts 1:13—*"And when they were come in, they went up into an upper room, where abode both Peter, and James, and John, and Andrew, Philip, and Thomas, Bartholomew, and Matthew, James the son of Alphaeus, and Simon Zelotes, and Judas the brother of James."* Two angels told the disciples Jesus would return the same way they saw Him go. The disciples followed Jesus' command and waited in Jerusalem for the Holy Spirit. They spent the time in prayer in one accord. Acts 1:14—*"These all continued with one accord in prayer and supplication, with the women, and Mary the mother of Jesus, and with his brethren."* The word abode in verse 13 tells us that they were in the Upper Room for ten days until Pentecost.

The Upper Room became a waiting room. Waiting goes against our flesh. Waiting upon the Lord would soon become their lifestyle. The Apostle Paul learned this very important lesson in ministry and taught others to do the same. Romans 12:7-9—*"Or ministry, let us wait on our ministering: or he that teacheth, on teaching; Or he that exhorteth, on exhortation: he that giveth, let him do it with simplicity; he that ruleth, with diligence; he that sheweth mercy, with cheerfulness. Let love be without dissimulation. Abhor that which is evil; cleave to that which is good."*

We have all been in God's waiting room. Have you ever been waiting for the doctor (someone who is going to try to help you) in a waiting room with other people? Let me ask you: How did you use your time waiting for the doctor? Will you use your time sleeping? People fall asleep while waiting. Some are "eyeball rollers." Every time another patient other than themselves is called, they roll their eyes. There is a complaint because the doctor is taking too long.

When I go to the doctor, I come prepared to wait. When waiting becomes your lifestyle, worry leaves, and the peace of God comes. Philippians 4:6-7—*"Be careful for nothing; but in every thing by prayer and supplication with thanksgiving let your requests be made known unto God. And the peace of God, which passeth all understanding, shall keep your hearts and minds through Christ Jesus."* Talk and listen to God in the waiting room. Keep your mind on the Lord in the waiting room. This waiting room was a crowded place. Remember, if we are in a waiting room, we are all waiting for the same purpose: to see the doctor. The Bible assures us of the benefits of waiting. Isaiah 40:31—*"But they that wait upon the Lord shall renew their strength; they shall mount up with wings as eagles; they shall run, and not be weary; and they shall walk, and not faint."* The word **"renew"** means **"exchange"** in this scripture. You exchange your weakness for His strength in waiting. Psalms 25:4-6—*"Shew me thy ways, O LORD; teach me thy paths. Lead me in thy truth, and teach me: for thou art the God of my salvation; on thee do I wait all the day. Remember, O LORD, thy tender mercies and thy lovingkindnesses; for they have been ever of old."* In waiting, we learn the ways of the Lord. In waiting, we learn the difference between our ways and His ways.

Isaiah 55:7-9—*"Let the wicked forsake his way, and the unrighteous man his thoughts: and let him return unto the LORD, and he will have mercy upon him; and to our God, for he will abundantly pardon. For my thoughts are not your thoughts, neither are your ways my ways, saith the LORD. For as the heavens are higher than the earth, so are my ways higher than your ways, and my thoughts than your thoughts."* In waiting, He will teach us His paths. His paths are a lifestyle of waiting on Him. Psalms 16:11—*"Thou wilt shew me the path of life: in thy presence is fulness of joy; at thy right hand there are pleasures for evermore."* While they waited for the Holy Ghost, they were learning to follow the truth.

There are many Psalms that encourage us to wait on God:

Psalms 4:4-5—*"Stand in awe, and sin not: commune with your own heart upon your bed, and be still. Selah. Offer the sacrifices of righteousness, and put your trust in the LORD."*

Psalms 27:13-14—*"I had fainted, unless I had believed to see the goodness of the LORD in the land of the living. Wait on the LORD: be of good courage, and he shall strengthen thine heart: wait, I say, on the LORD."*

Psalms 38:18-22—*"For I will declare mine iniquity; I will be sorry for my sin. But mine enemies are lively, and they are strong: and they that hate me wrongfully are multiplied. They also that render evil for good are mine adversaries; because I follow the thing that good is. Forsake me not, O LORD: O my God, be not far from me. Make haste to help me, O Lord my salvation."*

Psalms 37:34—*"Wait on the LORD, and keep his way, and he shall exalt thee to inherit the land: when the wicked are cut off, thou shalt see it."*

Psalms 52:9—*"I will praise thee for ever, because thou hast done it: and I will wait on thy name; for it is good before thy saints."*

Psalms 62:1-2—*"Truly my soul waiteth upon God: from him cometh my salvation. He only is my rock and my salvation; he is my defence; I shall not be greatly moved."*

Psalms 130:5-6—*"I wait for the LORD, my soul doth wait, and in his word do I hope. My soul waiteth for the Lord more than they that watch for the morning: I say, more than they that watch for the morning."*

Psalms 147:10-11—*"He delighteth not in the strength of the horse: he taketh not pleasure in the legs of a man. The LORD taketh pleasure in them that fear him, in those that hope in his mercy."*

If you jumped ahead of these verses to see what I would say next, go back. You haven't learned to wait yet. Remember what you are waiting for in each scripture I wrote. In Psalms 27, we learn about the goodness and courage of the Lord. In Psalms 37, we learn to inherit the land and the strength to keep His ways. In Psalms 52, His name.

In Psalms 62, we learn that there is solitude and stability in waiting. By waiting, He becomes our rock, our shield, and our salvation. In Psalms 130, while waiting, we will be in His Word. Waiting makes us alert and sensitive as to when God is speaking to us and directing us as watchmen.

Psalms 147 lets us know God doesn't take pleasure in what we do in our own strength. Favor comes to those who wait on the Lord.

While waiting, Peter, as the leader, gets into the Scriptures. Acts 1:15-20—*"And in those days Peter stood up in the midst of the disciples, and said, (the number of names together were about an hundred and twenty,) Men and brethren, this scripture must needs have been fulfilled, which the Holy Ghost by the mouth of David spake before concerning Judas, which was guide to them that took Jesus. For he was numbered with us, and had obtained part of this ministry. Now this man purchased a field with the reward of iniquity; and falling headlong, he burst asunder in the midst, and all his bowels gushed out. And it was known unto all the dwellers at Jerusalem; insomuch as that field is called in their proper tongue, Aceldama, that is to say, The field of blood. For it is written in the book of Psalms, Let his habitation be desolate, and let no man dwell therein: and his bishoprick let another take."*

Peter's purpose in addressing the disciples and others is to explain Judas' treachery and death in order to encourage them to choose a replacement for Judas. Some may have doubted what Peter said in verse 16. Peter mentions that the Holy Ghost spoke by the mouth of David concerning Judas. In verse 20, Peter quotes from Psalms 69:25—*"Let their habitation be desolate; and let none dwell in their tents."* Peter was led by the Holy Ghost to remember these verses. Peter understood something he had always missed. Fulfillment of Scripture was important.

John 13:18— *"I speak not of you all: I know whom I have chosen: but that the scripture may be fulfilled, He that eateth bread with me hath lifted up his heel against me."*

This is speaking of Judas walking away from Jesus and Judas' betrayal. To lift up your heel in their custom was to walk away permanently. To show your heel to someone was a great insult.

Peter, James, and John were close enough to hear Jesus say in John 17:12—*"While I was with them in the world, I kept them in thy name: those that thou gavest me I have kept, and none of them is lost, but the son of perdition; that the scripture might be fulfilled."* Judas' betrayal was the fulfillment of Scripture.

Peter, in seeking the fulfillment of Psalms 109:8, says—*"Let his days be few; and let another take his office."* He established the essential criteria for the one who would replace Judas as an apostle. He must be someone who has been an active disciple from the beginning of Jesus' ministry until His ascension. Acts 1:21-22—*"Wherefore of these men which have companied with us all the time that the Lord Jesus went in and out among us, Beginning from the baptism of John, unto that same day that he was taken up from us, must one be ordained to be a witness with us of his resurrection."*

They chose two candidates. The first was Joseph, known as Barsabbas (which means "son of the sabbath"), whose surname was Justus. The second was Matthias. Up until now, we had not heard of either of these men. Tradition says Matthias served later in Ethiopia.

Acts 1:24-26—*"And they prayed, and said, Thou, Lord, which knowest the hearts of all men, shew whether of these two thou hast chosen, That he may take part of this ministry and apostleship, from which Judas by transgression fell, that he might go to his own place. And they gave forth their lots; and the lot fell upon Matthias; and he was numbered with the eleven apostles."* They all prayed together.

In their prayer, they first acknowledged that they do not know everyone's heart. So, they asked the One who knows everyone's heart to show them which of the two He has chosen. God does not look outward, but at the heart.

They are asking God Himself to choose. Who is to take part in this ministry and apostleship: Matthias, whose name means "Gift of God." The choice was made by the disciples, who gave forth their lots. Their vote was not a gamble, but the same way they did later in Acts 15 at the Jerusalem Council. *"It seemed good unto us, being assembled with one accord, to send chosen men unto you with our beloved Barnabas and Paul, Men that have hazarded their lives for the name of our Lord Jesus Christ. We have sent therefore Judas and Silas, who shall also tell you the same things by mouth. For it seemed good to the Holy Ghost, and to us, to lay upon you no greater burden than these necessary things;"* (Acts 15:25-28)

James evaluated this new work of God among the Gentiles just as any work should be judged. James looked at what was written and quoted from Amos 9:11-12—*"In that day will I raise up the tabernacle of David that is fallen, and close up the breaches thereof; and I will raise up his ruins, and I will build it as in the days of old: That they may possess the remnant of Edom, and of all the heathen, which are called by my name, saith the LORD that doeth this."* Peter did the same in Acts 1:20.

CHAPTER 5

PENTECOST AND BEYOND

The meaning of Pentecost is God equipping His church with His Spirit so that He will be glorified among the nations. The purpose of Pentecost is to fulfill God's mission for the world.

Habakkuk 2:14—*"For the earth shall be filled with the knowledge of the glory of the LORD, as the waters cover the sea."*

If we truly understand Pentecost, our heart's burning desire will be to see every tribe, tongue, and nation bow before the exalted Lord Jesus Christ. God's plan for being glorified among the nations was to form the church, which He did on the Day of Pentecost.

If our hearts are not on world missions, our heart is not in tune with God's heart. To have His heart for the nation, we must have the Holy Spirit and walk in unity.

Acts 2:1-4— *"And when the day of Pentecost was fully come, they were all with one accord in one place. And suddenly there came a sound from heaven as of a rushing mighty wind, and it filled all the house where they were sitting. And there appeared unto them cloven tongues like as of fire, and it sat upon each of them. And they were all filled with the Holy Ghost, and began to speak with other tongues, as the Spirit gave them utterance."*

This was the initial experience of the feeling of the Holy Ghost on the Day of Pentecost. This was a Feast of the Lord held fifty days after the Feast of the Firstfruits during Passover and the time of Unleavened Bread. The first sheaf reaped from the harvest was waved unto God on the morrow after the Sabbath at the Feast of Firstfruits. Pentecost is called the Day of the Firstfruits.

Look at Numbers 28:26— *"Also in the day of the firstfruits, when ye bring a new meat offering unto the LORD, after your weeks be out, ye shall have an holy convocation; ye shall do no servile work:" Pentecost also marked the day the law was given to Israel. On the Old Testament Day of Pentecost, they received a law written on stone. It is a holy law that no one can ever keep because we are born with a stony heart. The law revealed to them that they were sinners in need of a savior. Ezekiel 36:26—"A new heart also will I give you, and a new spirit will I put within you: and I will take away the stony heart out of your flesh, and I will give you an heart of flesh." This is actually what happened on the Day of Pentecost: Jesus put a new heart* **(His heart)** *and a* **new spirit** *in them. When you receive the Holy Ghost, you are coming into covenant with the Lord; the baptism of the Holy Ghost is a sign of the covenant. He puts His laws in your new heart and mind. You receive Him by* **Grace**. *The Baptism of the Holy Ghost is the Spirit of Grace in its fullness.*

Leviticus 23:15-22— *"And ye shall count unto you from the morrow after the sabbath, from the day that ye brought the sheaf of the wave offering; seven sabbaths shall be complete: Even unto the morrow after the seventh sabbath shall ye number fifty days; and ye shall offer a new meat offering unto the LORD. Ye shall bring out of your habitations two wave loaves of two tenth deals; they shall be of fine flour; they shall be baken with leaven; they are the firstfruits unto the LORD. And ye shall offer with the bread seven lambs without blemish of the first year, and one young bullock, and two rams: they shall be for a burnt offering unto the LORD, with their meat offering, and their drink offerings, even an offering made by fire, of sweet savour unto the LORD. Then ye shall sacrifice one kid of the goats for a sin offering, and two lambs of the first year for a sacrifice of peace offerings. And the priest shall wave them with the bread of the firstfruits for a wave offering before the LORD, with the two lambs: they shall be holy to the LORD for the priest. And ye shall proclaim on the selfsame day, that it may be an holy convocation unto you: ye shall do no servile work therein: it shall be a statute for ever in all your dwellings throughout your generations. And when ye reap the harvest of your land, thou shalt not make clean riddance of the corners of thy field when thou reapest, neither shalt thou gather any gleaning of thy harvest: thou shalt leave them unto the poor, and to the stranger: I am the LORD your God."*

There are numerous Old Testament regulations on how to celebrate Pentecost. Take two loaves of leavened bread and wave them before the Lord. Signalizing that not only Israel shall be saved, but a multitude of the Gentiles shall come in. When the Day of Pentecost fully came, it was ten days after Jesus ascended to heaven, while they were still waiting in the Upper Room. Truly, the gift of the Holy Ghost is worth waiting for. It's a phenomenal gift, not earned but promised to us.

Acts 2:38-39— *"Then Peter said unto them, Repent, and be baptized every one of you in the name of Jesus Christ for the remission of sins, and ye shall receive the gift of the Holy Ghost. For the promise is unto you, and to your children, and to all that are afar off, even as many as the LORD our God shall call."*

It is not earned by our works but by seeking. They were all with one accord in one place. They were in one geographical place, with the same heart and love for God, and waiting for the same promise. By gathering together in prayer, we realize our own weaknesses. They, too, realized they could not do the task set before them without one another and the Holy Ghost.

As you read in Acts 2:2— *"And suddenly there came a sound from heaven as of a rushing mighty wind, and it filled all the house where they were sitting."*

In the Hebrew and Greek languages, the word for **"Spirit"** is the same word for "breath" or "wind." The "sound from heaven" was the sound of the Holy Spirit being breathed upon and into them. It was a mighty breathing sound. Genesis 2:7—*"And the LORD God formed man of the dust of the ground, and breathed into his nostrils the breath of life; and man became a living soul."*

It is the Spirit of God as the breath or wind of God, blowing life into man. In Acts, it was the Spirit of God as the breath or wind, blowing life into His new creations. We are recreated in Christ. 2 Corinthians 5:17—*"Therefore if any man be in Christ, he is a new creature: old things are passed away; behold, all things are become new."* Any man who is in **"Christ""** is a **"new creation."** When we are baptized in the Holy Ghost, we are "in Christ," submerged in the Holy Spirit. It is Christ in you, and you in Christ. Now they could understand John 15:4, where the Lord said, ***"Abide in me, and I in you."***

Malachi 3:1—*"Behold, I will send my messenger, and he shall prepare the way before me: and the LORD, whom ye seek, shall suddenly come to his temple, even the messenger of the covenant, whom ye delight in: behold, he shall come, saith the Lord of hosts."* The **"messenger of the covenant" is the Holy Spirit.** "They were sitting." Why? They could not stand in the presence of the Holy Ghost. Malachi 3:2—*"But who may abide the day of his coming? and who shall stand when he appeareth? for he is like a refiner's fire, and like fullers' soap:"* **It was a "mighty,"** rushing wind that came with great power. Again, look at Acts 2:3—*"And there appeared unto them cloven tongues like as of fire, and it sat upon each of them."*

John the Baptist prophesied that Jesus would baptize you with the Holy Ghost and with fire. Matthew 3:11—*"I indeed baptize you with water unto repentance. but he that cometh after me is mightier than I, whose shoes I am not worthy to bear: he shall* ***baptize you with the Holy Ghost, and with fire****:"* The picture of fire usually means purification, like a refiner's fire to make something pure. Malachi 3:1-4—*"Behold, I will send my messenger, and he shall prepare the way before me: and the LORD, whom ye seek, shall suddenly come to his temple, even the messenger of the covenant, whom ye delight in: behold, he shall come, saith the LORD of hosts. But who may abide the day of his coming? and who shall stand when he appeareth? for he is like a refiner's fire, and like fullers' soap: And he shall sit as a refiner and purifier of silver: and he shall purify the sons of Levi, and purge them as gold and silver, that they may offer unto the LORD an offering in righteousness. Then shall the offering of Judah and Jerusalem be pleasant unto the LORD, as in the days of old, and as in former years."* The Holy Spirit is not just for giving power but also for creating purity. Malachi 1:2—*"I have loved you, saith the LORD. Yet ye say, Wherein hast thou loved us? Was not Esau Jacob's brother? saith the LORD: yet I loved Jacob,"* The book of Malachi begins with a statement of how the covenant began—*"I have loved you."* This is what never changes about Jesus.

We need to always remember that. Malachi 3:6—*"For I am the LORD, I change not; therefore ye sons of Jacob are not consumed."* He loves us, and that never changes. That is the only reason the refiner's fire does not consume us but rather changes us. The Holy Ghost is a refiner's fire to change us, to remove the dross, and to refine us as pure gold. It didn't come as a forest fire to destroy us. A life lived by faith in the Holy Ghost and fire **purifies**.

1 Peter 1:6-7—*"Wherein ye greatly rejoice, though now for a season, if need be, ye are in heaviness through manifold temptations: That the trial of your faith, being much more precious than of gold that perisheth, though it be tried with fire, might be found unto praise and honour and glory at the appearing of Jesus Christ:"*

James 1:2-4—*"My brethren, count it all joy when ye fall into divers temptations; Knowing this, that the trying of your faith worketh patience. But let patience have her perfect work, that ye may be perfect and entire, wanting nothing."*

Romans 8:13—*"For if ye live after the flesh, ye shall die: but if ye through the Spirit do mortify the deeds of the body, ye shall live."* By yielding to the "cloven tongues like as of fire," we are purified. A fire must have air to breathe, fuel (disciples) to burn, and wind to spread, and spread it did, all in one day.

Acts 2:41—*"Then they that gladly received his word were baptized: and the same day there were added unto them about three thousand souls."*

Let us look at what happened in Acts and compare it with the giving of the law on Sinai. Hebrews 12:18-19—*"For ye are not come unto the mount that might be touched, and that burned with fire, nor unto blackness, and darkness, and tempest, And the sound of a trumpet, and the voice of words; which voice they that heard intreated that the word should not be spoken to them any more:"* This verse mentions the "fire, tempest (wind), and voice of words (tongue)," at the inauguration of the Mosaic dispensation. Something similar to what they witnessed at Pentecost, but without blackness, darkness, or terror in the people.

Exodus 19:16-18— *"And it came to pass on the third day in the morning, that there were thunders and lightnings, and a thick cloud upon the mount, and the voice of the trumpet exceeding loud; so that all the people that was in the camp trembled. And Moses brought forth the people out of the camp to meet with God; and they stood at the nether part of the mount. And mount Sinai was altogether on a smoke, because the Lord descended upon it in fire: and the smoke thereof ascended as the smoke of a furnace, and the whole mount quaked greatly." They were in the Upper Room on Mt. Sion, not Sinai.*

Hebrews 12:22-29— "But ye are come unto mount Sion, and unto the city of the living God, the heavenly Jerusalem, and to an innumerable company of angels, To the general assembly and church of the firstborn, which are written in heaven, and to God the Judge of all, and to the spirits of just men made perfect, And to Jesus the mediator of the new covenant, and to the blood of sprinkling, that speaketh better things than that of Abel. See that ye refuse not him that speaketh. For if they escaped not who refused him that spake on earth, much more shall not we escape, if we turn away from him that speaketh from heaven: Whose voice then shook the earth: but now he hath promised, saying, Yet once more I shake not the earth only, but also heaven. And this word, Yet once more, signifieth the removing of those things that are shaken, as of things that are made, that those things which cannot be shaken may remain. Wherefore we receiving a kingdom which cannot be moved, let us have grace, whereby we may serve God acceptably with reverence and godly fear: For our God is a consuming fire." What they entered into was a heavenly Jerusalem and a spiritual Kingdom—a Kingdom that cannot be shaken. I will have more on that in my next book.

Looking back to the "fire" in Acts, they saw something that looked like fire. Fire purifies and consumes the chaff. Matthew 3:12—*"Whose fan is in his hand, and he will throughly purge his floor, and gather his wheat into the garner; but he will burn up the chaff with unquenchable fire."* The remnants of the old man. Look at the parallels in this verse: fan (wind), floor (Upper Room), wheat (Pentecost), the harvest of the wheat (believers), and consuming fire (tongues of fire). All the disciples were experiencing what Jeremiah experienced. Jeremiah 20:9—*"Then I said, I will not make mention of him, nor speak any more in his name. But his word was in mine heart as a burning fire shut up in my bones, and I was weary with forbearing, and I could not stay."* From this day forth, the words of Jesus were fire in their bones. We need Holy Ghost fire. Our God is a consuming fire. A consuming fire, if it is set on any item, will not be quenched without fully consuming that item.

Deuteronomy 4:24—*"For the LORD thy God is a consuming fire, even a jealous God."* Hebrews 12:29—*"For our God is a consuming fire."* The Holy Ghost is a consuming fire. Hebrews 13:1—*"Let brotherly love continue."* The only thing left after the consuming fire is brotherly love.

Some ask, "Is speaking in tongues for everyone?" I believe the answer is, "Yes." Acts 2:39—*"For the promise is unto you, and to your children, and to all that are afar off, even as many as the LORD our God shall call."*

On three occasions in the book of Acts, speaking in tongues is accompanied by the receiving of the Holy Ghost. Again, look at Acts 2:4—*"And they were all filled with the Holy Ghost, and began to speak with other tongues, as the Spirit gave them utterance."* Acts 10:43-46—*"To him give all the prophets witness, that through his name whosoever believeth in him shall receive remission of sins. While Peter yet spake these words, the Holy Ghost fell on all them which heard the word. And they of the circumcision which believed were astonished, as many as came with Peter, because that on the Gentiles also was poured out the gift of the Holy Ghost. For they heard them speak with tongues, and magnify God. Then answered Peter,"* Acts 19:6—*"And when Paul had laid his hands upon them, the Holy Ghost came on them; and they spake with tongues, and prophesied."*

Some ask, "Is speaking in tongues evidence of receiving the Holy Ghost?" My answer is, "No," but it is a sign. The true evidence is the Fruits of the Spirit. Galatians 5:22-23—***"But the fruit of the Spirit is love, joy, peace, longsuffering, gentleness, goodness, faith, Meekness, temperance: against such there is no law."***

Please, Pastors, never forbid speaking in tongues. 1 Corinthians 14:39—*"Wherefore, brethren, covet to prophesy, and forbid not to speak with tongues."* But to those of you who manifest tongues, don't let your flesh get involved. It must be done decently and in order. The Holy Ghost came because of obedience, and tongues followed His indwelling. Acts 5:32—*"And we are his witnesses of these things; and so is also the Holy Ghost, whom God hath given to them that obey him."* Acts 8:15-17—*"Who, when they were come down, prayed for them, that they might receive the Holy Ghost: (For as yet he was fallen upon none of them: only they were baptized in the name of the Lord Jesus.) Then laid they their hands on them, and they received the Holy Ghost."* That lets us know tongues are an experience after salvation.

Now read Acts 19:3-6—*"And he said unto them, Unto what then were ye baptized? And they said, Unto John's baptism. Then said Paul, John verily baptized with the baptism of repentance, saying unto the people, that they should believe on him which should come after him, that is, on Christ Jesus. When they heard this, they were baptized in the name of the Lord Jesus. And when Paul had laid his hands upon them, the Holy Ghost came on them; and they spake with tongues, and prophesied."* I thought these scriptures were important to mention again because the sign they received was speaking in tongues. But the evidence of the infilling comes later with the Fruit of the Spirit. Speaking in tongues is the first manifestation sign of the infilling of the Holy Ghost.

I say it this way because I have seen men fake speaking in tongues, but I like to say you can't fake the Fruit of the Spirit. There isn't a scripture where the Bible records people speaking in tongues, except where people were filled with the Holy Ghost.

Some people use the following verses against those who speak in an unknown tongue:

Acts 2:5-8—*"And there were dwelling at Jerusalem Jews, devout men, out of every nation under heaven. Now when this was noised abroad, the multitude came together, and were confounded, because that every man heard them speak in his own language. And they were all amazed and marvelled, saying one to another, Behold, are not all these which speak Galilaeans? And how hear we every man in our own tongue, wherein we were born?"*

I want to give one verse that will make my viewpoint clear: 1 Corinthians 13:1—*"Though I speak with the tongues of men and of angels, and have not charity, I am become as sounding brass, or a tinkling cymbal."* Again, when the Holy Spirit burns off the chaff, the only thing left is love; Christ's love working through us.

Acts 2:14-15— *"But Peter, standing up with the eleven, lifted up his voice, and said unto them, Ye men of Judaea, and all ye that dwell at Jerusalem, be this known unto you, and hearken to my words: For these are not drunken, as ye suppose, seeing it is but the third hour of the day."*

Peter stands up with the eleven to preach. They were all still in one accord. Peter raised or lifted up his voice. Peter is filled with courage and boldness, unlike when he denied Jesus before being filled with the Holy Ghost. Peter didn't do as the Rabbis of that day would, who would sit down and instruct those listening. Peter boldly proclaimed the truth.

Acts 2:13— *"Others mocking said, These men are full of new wine."*

In this scripture, Peter answered those who mocked and criticized, saying they were drunk. Peter communicated that it is not even thinkable that people would be so drunk early in the day; the third hour is 9:00 in the morning. The custom of the Jews was not to eat or drink anything until after the hour of prayer, which is when the Holy Spirit filled the house, which is seen in Acts 3:1.

Acts 2:16-21— *"But this is that which was spoken by the prophet Joel; And it shall come to pass in the last days, saith God, I will pour out of my Spirit upon all flesh: and your sons and your daughters shall prophesy, and your young men shall see visions, and your old men shall dream dreams: And on my servants and on my handmaidens I will pour out in those days of my Spirit; and they shall prophesy: And I will shew wonders in heaven above, and signs in the earth beneath; blood, and fire, and vapour of smoke: The sun shall be turned into darkness, and the moon into blood, before the great and notable day of the Lord come: And it shall come to pass, that whosoever shall call on the name of the Lord shall be saved."*

In the middle of a great outpouring of the Holy Ghost with signs, wonders, and speaking in tongues, Peter pauses and says, "Let's go to the book of Joel." I hear some people say, "We had a great service, and nobody even preached." This bothers me.

All the signs, wonders, and speaking in tongues were preparing them for what Peter was about to share from God's Word, which, by the way, resulted in a huge altar call that added to them three thousand souls. Some think it is more spiritual if there is no Word brought forth. Others think if the Word is brought forth, and there are no signs or wonders, then they are more spiritual or mature. They are both wrong. The Spirit and the Word agree.

Peter quotes from the prophet Joel. Joel 2:28-32—*"And it shall come to pass afterward, that I will pour out my spirit upon all flesh; and your sons and your daughters shall prophesy, your old men shall dream dreams, your young men shall see visions: And also upon the servants and upon the handmaids in those days will I pour out my spirit. And I will shew wonders in the heavens and in the earth, blood, and fire, and pillars of smoke. The sun shall be turned into darkness, and the moon into blood, before the great and terrible day of the LORD come. And it shall come to pass, that whosoever shall call on the name of the LORD shall be delivered: for in mount Zion and in Jerusalem shall be deliverance, as the Lord hath said, and in the remnant whom the LORD shall call."*

Part of this prophecy was fulfilled on Pentecost, with the other being fulfilled in the last days. The fulfillment is still Jesus' coming. Prophet Joel says, "Afterwards," but Peter says, "This is that which was spoken by the Prophet Joel." This was a glorious message brought forth on the Day of Pentecost. Under the Old Covenant, only certain people were moved upon by the Spirit at various times for specific purposes. Now, under the New Covenant, the outpouring of the Holy Ghost is for everyone who calls upon the name of the LORD!

Let's look at Peter's sermon. I recommend taking a few minutes to read through the whole thing. Acts 2:22-41— *"Ye men of Israel, hear these words; Jesus of Nazareth, a man approved of God among you by miracles and wonders and signs, which God did by him in the midst of you, as ye yourselves also know: Him, being delivered by the determinate counsel and foreknowledge of God, ye have taken, and by wicked hands have crucified and slain: Whom God hath raised up, having loosed the pains of death: because it was not possible that he should be holden of it. For David speaketh concerning him, I foresaw the Lord always before my face, for he is on my right hand, that I should not be moved: Therefore did my heart rejoice, and my tongue was glad; moreover also my flesh shall rest in hope: Because thou wilt not leave my soul in hell, neither wilt thou suffer thine Holy One to see corruption. Thou hast made known to me the ways of life; thou shalt make me full of joy with thy countenance. Men and brethren, let me freely speak unto you of the patriarch David, that he is both dead and buried, and his sepulchre is with us unto this day. Therefore being a prophet, and knowing that God had sworn with an oath to him, that of the fruit of his loins, according to the flesh, he would raise up Christ to sit on his throne; He seeing this before spake of the resurrection of Christ, that his soul was not left in hell, neither his flesh did see corruption.*

This Jesus hath God raised up, whereof we all are witnesses. Therefore being by the right hand of God exalted, and having received of the Father the promise of the Holy Ghost, he hath shed forth this, which ye now see and hear. For David is not ascended into the heavens: but he saith himself, The Lord said unto my Lord, Sit thou on my right hand, Until I make thy foes thy footstool. Therefore let all the house of Israel know assuredly, that God hath made the same Jesus, whom ye have crucified, both Lord and Christ. Now when they heard this, they were pricked in their heart, and said unto Peter and to the rest of the apostles, Men and brethren, what shall we do? Then Peter said unto them, Repent, and be baptized every one of you in the name of Jesus Christ for the remission of sins, and ye shall receive the gift of the Holy Ghost.

For the promise is unto you, and to your children, and to all that are afar off, even as many as the LORD our God shall call. And with many other words did he testify and exhort, saying, Save yourselves from this untoward generation. Then they that gladly received his word were baptized: and the same day there were added unto them about three thousand souls." Peter is preaching to unbelievers. Jesus had clearly given the disciples a mandate to preach the Gospel to the whole world for the salvation of souls.

Matthew 28:18-20— *"And Jesus came and spake unto them, saying, All power is given unto me in heaven and in earth. Go ye therefore, and teach all nations, baptizing them in the name of the Father, and of the Son, and of the Holy Ghost: Teaching them to observe all things whatsoever I have commanded you: and, lo, I am with you always, even unto the end of the world. Amen."*

Mark 16:15-20— *"And he said unto them, Go ye into all the world, and preach the gospel to every creature. He that believeth and is baptized shall be saved; but he that believeth not shall be damned. And these signs shall follow them that believe; In my name shall they cast out devils; they shall speak with new tongues; They shall take up serpents; and if they drink any deadly thing, it shall not hurt them; they shall lay hands on the sick, and they shall recover. So then after the Lord had spoken unto them, he was received up into heaven, and sat on the right hand of God. And they went forth, and preached every where, the Lord working with them, and confirming the word with signs following. Amen."*

Pentecost is often called the "Birthday of the Church," because it is on that day that the apostles, strengthened by the Holy Spirit, started to preach the Gospel of Jesus Christ to the whole world.

Notice that the responsibility of the Church isn't to make people feel comfortable about themselves or even simply to exhort our fellow Christians.

Our main responsibility is going out in the streets and preaching the Gospel to people who are not already saved. Peter is quoting extensively from the Scripture in his sermon. We must stay in the Word to fulfill Christ's mandates. Peter is preaching from the Old Testament; the New Testament was not written yet. Some preachers today refuse to preach from the Old Testament, but I would like to point something out. Not only is it just as inspired as the New Testament, but the Old Testament preaches Christ and is indispensable for understanding the Gospel of Jesus Christ in its fullness.

"Think not that I am come to destroy the law, or the prophets: I am not come to destroy, but to fulfil."
(Matthew 5:17)

Therefore, let all the house of Israel know assuredly that God has made this Jesus, whom you crucified, both Lord and Christ

Peter openly confronted them with their sin in Acts 2:23 (NKJV)—*"Him, being delivered by the determined purpose and foreknowledge of God, you have taken by lawless hands, have crucified, and put to death."* Peter declared unto them in Acts 2:36 (NKJV)—*"...God has made this Jesus, whom you crucified, both Lord and Christ."*

Modern-day preachers would say that Peter was being too harsh. By openly pointing out the people's sin and its consequences, surely, they will turn people off to Jesus. They think Peter should stay positive and only talk about how much Jesus loves them. Please listen, except that you understand you are a sinner that needs saving; you cannot accept the Gospel! Salvation from our sins is precisely what the Gospel is! Jesus' very name means **"God saves"** in Hebrew. It was given to Him "because He will save his people from their sins."

Matthew 1:21—*"And she shall bring forth a son, and thou shalt call his name JESUS: for he shall save his people from their sins."* If people don't know that they are sinners in desperate need of God's grace for salvation, then it won't be clear why they need Jesus at all in the first place. After hearing Peter clearly preach about their sinfulness and about Christ's death, resurrection, and ascension into heaven, Peter replied, as you read in Acts 2:38, saying—*"Then Peter said unto them, Repent, and be baptized every one of you in the name of Jesus Christ for the remission of sins, and ye shall receive the gift of the Holy Ghost."*

Peter tells them to do two things: to repent of their sins and to be baptized. Remember what they needed to do? Acts 2:40 told us—*"And with many other words did he testify and exhort, saying, Save yourselves from this untoward generation."*

Peter doesn't spend any time trying to win people over by telling them how great they are. This world is fallen, and the life Christ calls us to demands change. If you are living the way most people around you are living, you are probably not following Jesus. This is why Peter preached, *"Save yourselves from this untoward (corrupt) generation."* We see in Acts 2:41 that after Peter's sermon, 3,000 people were converted in one day.

Let's understand Acts 2:42-45— *"And they continued stedfastly in the apostles' doctrine and fellowship, and in breaking of bread, and in prayers. And fear came upon every soul: and many wonders and signs were done by the apostles. And all that believed were together, and had all things common; And sold their possessions and goods, and parted them to all men, as every man had need."*

It says, *"They continued steadfastly,"* which is similar to the Greek word "proskarterountes," which can mean "to be earnest, to persevere, to be constantly diligent, or to adhere closely to." This is the same word that Luke used to describe the activities of the disciples following Jesus' ascension when Luke said in Acts 1:14—*"These all continued with one accord in prayer and supplication."*

Let's talk about the apostles' doctrine. You may ask what the Apostles' Doctrine is. The word "doctrine" derives from the Latin term for teaching. It refers to the content that was taught in the New Testament. The proper teaching of Scripture was called "The apostles' doctrine," meaning that which the apostles taught. They only taught what Jesus taught them. The apostles' doctrine is true not because an apostle said it but because it is "consistent" with what the whole Word of God says.

The Bereans examined the teachings of Paul in light of the Scriptures before accepting it. Acts 17:10-12—*"And the brethren immediately sent away Paul and Silas by night unto Berea: who coming thither went into the synagogue of the Jews. These were more noble than those in Thessalonica, in that they received the word with all readiness of mind, and searched the scriptures daily, whether those things were so. Therefore many of them believed; also of honourable women which were Greeks, and of men, not a few."*

They continued in "**fellowship**." The term Luke uses for fellowship is a much broader term than our English word. Essentially, fellowship means "joint participation" or "sharing something in common." It is thus a kind of partnership. Philippians 2:1-2—*"If there be therefore any consolation in Christ, if any comfort of love, if any fellowship of the Spirit, if any bowels and mercies, Fulfil ye my joy, that ye be likeminded, having the same love, being of one accord, of one mind."* The term used for fellowship is a common sharing together in the Holy Spirit.

The apostles broke bread from house to house. They continued with the breaking of bread and prayers. This "breaking of bread" is included with the teaching and the prayers. It's an activity of faith and worship to which they devoted themselves. It is clear that "breaking of bread" in that context is a reference to the Communion Supper that Jesus instituted the night He was betrayed.

We find what appears to be another breaking of bread in Acts 2:46—*"And they, continuing daily with one accord in the temple, and breaking bread from house to house, did eat their meat with gladness and singleness of heart,"* Here, for the disciples, "breaking bread" is defined as eating meals together. So, in the Early Church, we find them "breaking bread" in two distinct activities.

Finally, Acts 2:47—*"Praising God, and having favour with all the people. And the Lord added to the church daily such as should be saved."* We are going to end this study with this verse. I long to see Acts 2 in the church again, and we will see this again as we personally and corporately take to heart the truths, the principles, and the love with which I presented them to you.

CHAPTER 6

ROSH HASHANAH, "THE TRUMPET FEAST"

The "casting off" is a ceremony performed on the afternoon of the first day of Rosh Hashanah.

During this ceremony, Jews symbolically cast off the sins of the previous year by tossing pebbles or breadcrumbs into flowing water (living water). Jesus has cast all our sins into the depths of the sea.

Despite all the sins that His people have committed, even when they provoked Him to so much anger, God will not cancel out His covenant with His people.

Instead, He will be merciful and compassionate to them when they turn to Him in repentance. Micah 7:19—*"He will turn again, he will have compassion upon us; he will subdue our iniquities; and thou wilt cast all their sins into the depths of the sea."* Ecclesiastes 11:1—*"Cast thy bread upon the waters: for thou shalt find it after many days."*

Rosh Hashanah (Feast of Trumpets) is a two-day celebration. The narrative in the Book of Genesis describing the announcement of Isaac's birth and his subsequent birth is part of the Torah readings in synagogues on the first day of Rosh Hashanah, and the narrative of the sacrifice and binding of Isaac is read in the synagogue on the second day of Rosh Hashanah!

I am fully convinced Jesus was born on the first of Rosh Hashanah and will return in all of His Glory on the first of Sukkot (Feast of Tabernacles).

The shofar is sounded one hundred times during a traditional Rosh Hashanah service.

A long and loud shofar blast marks the end of the fast day of Yom Kippur. While the blower must first take a big breath, the shofar only sounds when the air blows out.

This is a symbol for Rosh Hashanah: we must turn inward to examine ourselves so we can then burst out (by the breath of God) and contribute to the world through the Holy Spirit.

We are the Shofar. The Holy Spirit is the breath!

THE LAST DAY OF AWE

The last Day of Awe was a fast day, the holiest day of the year, Yom Kippur, or Day of Atonement. The Day of Judgment was when God would judge mankind from His throne (Mercy Seat).

For on this day, He will forgive you, to purify you, that you be cleansed from all your sins before God. The blood is still on the Mercy Seat. You will never be able to stand before the throne without the blood. The two cherubim no longer hold the flaming sword barring our entrance to the Garden of Eden.

They face toward each other. They look down upon the blood on the Mercy Seat of God. They see each other's reflections through the blood. That speaks volumes to me.

We must see each other through the blood. Eternal life, hidden with Christ in God, is ours through faith in Jesus. Jesus is not only the blood on the Mercy Seat; He is the Mercy Seat.

The Day of Atonement can be referred to as the Day of Redemption, the Day of Purification, or the Day of Reconciliation. This day was and is very important to every Jewish believer because it is a reminder that, one day, they will be reconciled with their God. Jesus had already done it for us.

Zechariah 3:9—*"For behold the stone that I have laid before Joshua; upon one stone shall be seven eyes: behold, I will engrave the graving thereof, saith the LORD of hosts, and I will remove the iniquity of that land in* ***one day****."*

Hebrews 10:16-26—*"This is the covenant that I will make with them after those days, saith the Lord, I will put my laws into their hearts, and in their minds will I write them; And their sins and iniquities will I remember no more. Now where remission of these is, there is no more offering for sin. Having therefore, brethren, boldness to enter into the holiest by the blood of Jesus, By a new and living way, which he hath consecrated for us, through the veil, that is to say, his flesh; And having an high priest over the house of God; Let us draw near with a true heart in full assurance of faith, having our hearts sprinkled from an evil conscience, and our bodies washed with pure water. Let us hold fast the profession of our faith without wavering; (for he is faithful that promised;) And let us consider one another to provoke unto love and to good works: Not forsaking the assembling of ourselves together, as the manner of some is; but exhorting one another: and so much the more, as ye see the day approaching. For if we sin wilfully after that we have received the knowledge of the truth, there remaineth no more sacrifice for sins,"*

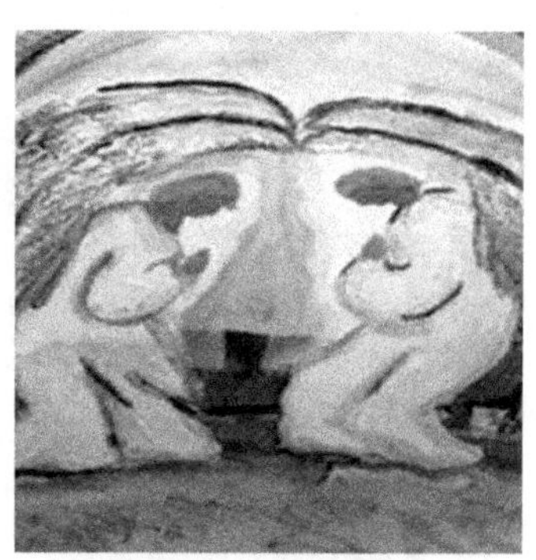

Jesus' sacrifice on the cross forgives us of sin! He also gave us the answer to our sin nature by putting His law in our hearts and minds!

Now we can come boldly to His Throne (the Mercy Seat) to get help to live a new and living way.

He paid for us not to just forgive our sins and the blood of the first goat to be sprinkled on the Mercy Seat but also for the scapegoat and that our sin nature be removed far from us.

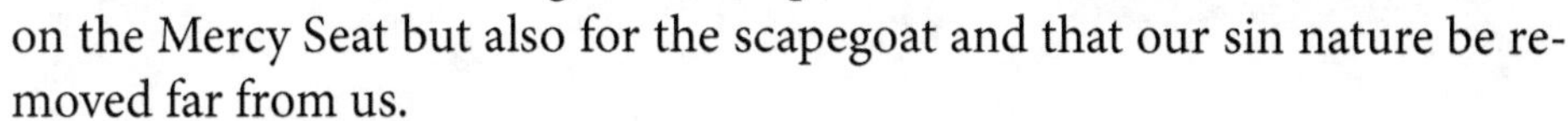

Psalms 103:12—"*As far as the east is from the west, so far hath he removed our transgressions from us.*"

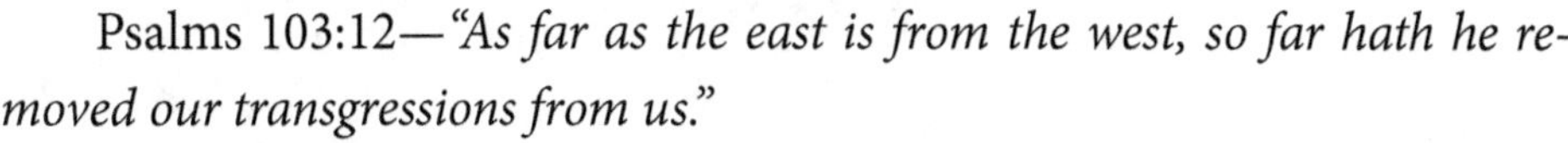

CHAPTER 7

GREAT HOSANNA

The Feast of Tabernacles was a season of great rejoicing, and it was a saying amongst the Jews that those who had not witnessed it did not know what joy meant. In this way, Hosanna became associated with rejoicing. The same must be said of the use of palm branches! For the first six days, the priests walked around the altar while rehearsing Psalms 118:25. On the 7th day, the last day of Tabernacles, the people, not just the priests, would circle the altar seven times, waving palm branches, marking that a new day had come.

Psalms 118:25-26—*"Save now, I beseech thee, O LORD: O LORD, I beseech thee, send now prosperity. Blessed be he that cometh in the name of the LORD: we have blessed you out of the house of the LORD."*

Isaiah 25:1-9—*"O Lord, thou art my God; I will exalt thee, I will praise thy name; for thou hast done wonderful things; thy counsels of old are faithfulness and truth. For thou hast made of a city an heap; of a defenced city a ruin: a palace of strangers to be no city; it shall never be built. Therefore shall the strong people glorify thee, the city of the terrible nations shall fear thee. For thou hast been a strength to the poor, a strength to the needy in his distress, a refuge from the storm, a shadow from the heat, when the blast of the terrible ones is as a storm against the wall. Thou shalt bring down the noise of strangers, as the heat in a dry place; even the heat with the shadow of a cloud: the branch of the terrible ones shall be brought low. And in this mountain shall the LORD of hosts make unto all people a feast of fat things, a feast of wines on the lees, of fat things full of marrow, of wines on the lees well refined.* **(Feast of Tabernacles)**

And he will destroy in this mountain the face of the covering cast over all people, and the vail that is spread over all nations. He will swallow up death in victory; and the Lord GOD will wipe away tears from off all faces; and the rebuke of his people shall he take away from off all the earth: for the Lord hath spoken it.

And it shall be said in that day, Lo, this is our God; we have waited for him, and he will save us: this is the LORD; we have waited for him, we will be glad and rejoice in his salvation."

(GREAT HOSANNA) (REDEMPTION OF THE WHOLE MAN SPIRIT SOUL AND BODY)

John 7:2—*"Now the Jew's feast of tabernacles was at hand."*

John 7:37-39—*"In the last day, that great day of the feast,* **(GREAT HOSANNA)** *Jesus stood and cried, saying, If any man thirst, let him come unto me, and drink. He that believeth on me, as the scripture hath said, out of his belly shall flow rivers of living water. (But this spake he of the Spirit, which they that believe on him should receive: for the Holy Ghost was not yet given; because that Jesus was not yet glorified.)*

THE WATER-DRAWING FESTIVAL

The priests would go down to the pool of Siloam in the City of David (just south of where the Western Wall is today), and they would fill a golden vessel with the water there. They would go up to the temple through the Water Gate, accompanied by the sound of the shofar, and then they would pour the water so that it flowed over the altar, along with wine from another bowl called the **Living Water**. This would begin the prayers for rain in earnest, and there was much rejoicing at this ceremony. They would recite Psalms 118. The ceremony also refers to this passage in Isaiah 12:2-3—*"Behold, God is my salvation; I will trust, and not be afraid: for the LORD JEHOVAH is my strength and my song; he also is become my salvation. Therefore with joy shall ye draw water out of the wells of salvation."*

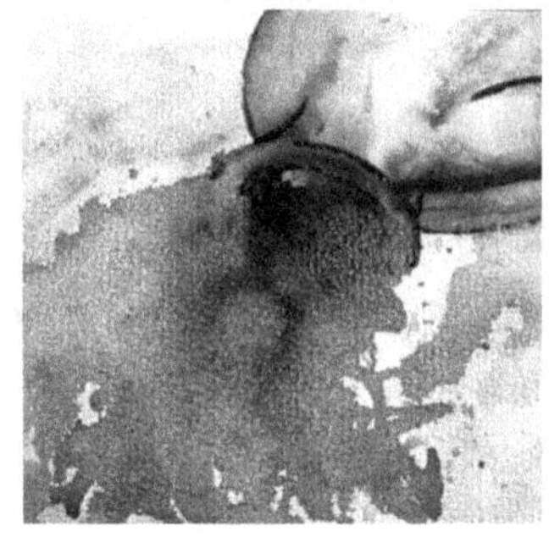

You may already know that this is the exact word of Yeshua's name: **Salvation**. The Hebrew word literally says with joy, you will draw water from the wells of Yeshua (**Salvation**).

Revelation 22:17—*"And the Spirit and the bride say, Come. And let him that heareth say, Come. And let him that is athirst come. And whosoever will, let him take the water of life freely."*

John 8:1-2—*"Jesus went unto the mount of Olives. And early in the morning he came again into the temple, and all the people came unto him; and he sat down, and taught them."* **(It is still the last because the day begins in the Bible in the evening and morning.)**

NOTICE WHAT HAPPENED NEXT

John 8:3-12—*"And the scribes and Pharisees brought unto him a woman taken in adultery; and when they had set her in the midst, They say unto him, Master, this woman was taken in adultery, in the very act. Now Moses in the law commanded us, that such should be stoned: but what sayest thou? This they said, tempting him, that they might have to accuse him. But Jesus stooped down, and with his finger wrote on the ground, as though he heard them not. So when they continued asking him, he lifted up himself, and said unto them, He that is without sin among you, let him first cast a stone at her. And again he stooped down, and wrote on the ground. And they which heard it, being convicted by their own conscience, went out one by one, beginning at the eldest, even unto the last: and Jesus was left alone, and the woman standing in the midst. When Jesus had lifted up himself, and saw none but the woman, he said unto her, Woman, where are those thine accusers? hath no man condemned thee? She said, No man, Lord. And Jesus said unto her, Neither do I condemn thee: go, and sin no more. Then spake Jesus again unto them, saying, I am the light of the world: he that followeth me shall not walk in darkness, but shall have the light of life."*

I am convinced Jesus wrote Jeremiah 17:13—*"O LORD, the hope of Israel, all that forsake thee shall be ashamed, and they that depart from me shall be written in the earth, because they have forsaken the LORD, the fountain of living waters."*

I believe Jesus wrote the Ten Commandments down on the ground first, then when He wrote the second time, He wrote their names beside the Commandment they had been breaking. Jesus writes the law not on stone this time, but on the ground, on the very dirt from which Adam was made in creation. The heart is the first organ to form during development of the body in the womb. I believe the first thing God created in Adam was the heart of man.

Her accusers all walked away in shame because the **light** exposed their sin, and they loved darkness rather than light. Jesus did not come to condemn the world, but that the world might be saved. Jesus never condemned the woman but warned her to sin no more.

The Feast of Tabernacles continues in John 9. Blindness and sight are mentioned in 24 of the chapter's 41 verses, including the first and last ones. The details of the miracle itself are repeated four times: that Jesus put mud on the eyes of the blind man, and then he regained his sight.

The story here is still during the Feast of Tabernacles, which is the setting for chapters 7 and 8. The Pool of Siloam, where the man born blind is sent to wash his eyes, figures in water ceremonies at the festival, and Jesus has already invited the thirsty to come to Him and drink on the great day of the feast in John 7:37-38.

Light was also an important theme, and Jesus declares himself the light of the world at the feast in John 8:12, and again here in John 9:5—*"As long as I am in the world, I am the light of the world."* I believe Jesus used mud because He knew the High Sabbath (the last day of the feast, not the weekly Sabbath), and it's against the law to knead dough, clay, or mud. According to the interpretations of the Pharisees as to what it means not to work on the Sabbath, the Hebrew word for "dough" is identical (pēlos) to the word "mud" or "clay." It's like brick masons saying, "Give me some more mud" (moldable cement); it's the same word.

Jesus knew exactly what He was doing: "I'm going to break their law—not the law God gave but man's interpretation, which has always been the problem." I can't begin to imagine why anyone would get upset because the blind man was healed. Look at even His disciples in John 9:1-3—*"And as Jesus passed by, he saw a man which was blind from his birth. And his disciples asked him, saying, Master, who did sin, this man, or his parents, that he was born blind? Jesus answered, Neither hath this man sinned, nor his parents: but that the works of God should be made manifest in him."*

Jesus's disciples showed no interest in helping the blind man but in discussing the cause of his condition. James 5:14-16—*"Is any sick among you? let him call for the elders of the church; and let them pray over him, anointing him with oil in the name of the Lord: And the prayer of faith shall save the sick, and the Lord shall raise him up; and if he have committed sins, they shall be forgiven him. Confess your faults one to another, and pray one for another, that ye may be healed. The effectual fervent prayer of a righteous man availeth much."*

God's people, oftentimes, instead of moving with love and compassion towards sinners or even the sick, move with a judgmental spirit.

God, help the Church to move with Your love and compassion.

CHAPTER 8

PSALMS OF ASCENT

Psalms 120-134 were called Psalms of Ascent or Degrees! What are the Songs of Ascent or Degrees in the Book of Psalms? This is the title given to fifteen Psalms: 120-134.

The word is maalah, which signifies "going up, ascent" and is translated as "stairs, steps, going up." These Psalms have been grouped together: four are by David, one by Solomon, and the rest are without a name. The Psalms (or Songs) of Ascent were always sung at the night or evening service of Succoth or the Feast of Tabernacles. We need to realize Jesus in the Seven Feasts of the Lord.

THE FEASTS

Leviticus 23 briefly covers all of the Feasts of the Lord. There are three annual feasts that the Lord commanded all of Israel to celebrate in Jerusalem: Passover, Shavuot (Pentecost), and Sukkot (Feast of Tabernacles). Each of these feasts, regardless of when or how it is celebrated, is called the same thing: a "holy convocation." Look at Isaiah 1:11-19—*"To what purpose is the multitude of your sacrifices unto me? saith the LORD: I am full of the burnt offerings of rams, and the fat of fed beasts; and I delight not in the blood of bullocks, or of lambs, or of he goats. When ye come to appear before me, who hath required this at your hand, to tread my courts? Bring no more vain oblations; incense is an abomination unto me; the new moons and sabbaths, the calling of assemblies, I cannot away with; it is iniquity, even the solemn meeting. Your new moons and your appointed feasts my soul hateth: they are a trouble unto me; I am weary to bear them. And when ye spread forth your hands, I will hide mine eyes from you: yea, when ye make many prayers, I will not hear: your hands are full of blood. Wash you, make you clean; put away the evil of your doings from before mine eyes; cease to do evil; Learn to do well; seek judgment, relieve the oppressed, judge the fatherless, plead for the widow. Come now, and let us reason together, saith the LORD: though your sins be as scarlet, they shall be as white as snow; though they be red like crimson, they shall be as wool. If ye be willing and obedient, ye shall eat the good of the land:"*

God despised THEIR FEASTS OR APPOINTED TIMES, according to Isaiah 1. John 7:2 CALLS IT THE FEAST OF THE JEWS. Why did He hate their feast day? Because it was no longer the Lord's feast but Israel's feast instead. We have done the same today and substituted the Lord's feast for the pagan feast! Passover, Unleavened Bread, Firstfruits, and Pentecost—Jesus fulfilled all four of these feasts. That didn't do away with them, but they became a continuous feast. We can partake of them anytime or seasonally if our hearts are after the feasting of the Lord.

Proverbs 15:15-17—*"All the days of the afflicted are evil: but he that is of a* ***merry heart*** *hath a* ***continual feast****. Better is little with the fear of the Lord than great treasure and trouble therewith. Better is a dinner of herbs where love is, than a stalled ox and hatred therewith."*

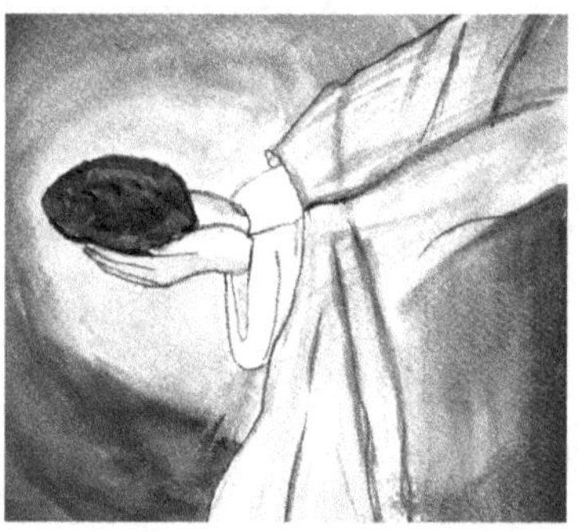

Jesus didn't replace or do away with them, nor did the early church. Apostle Paul says in 1 Corinthians 16:8—*"But I will tarry at Ephesus until Pentecost."* Here, Paul is keeping this feast in Ephesus. Acts 20:16—*"For Paul had determined to sail by Ephesus, because he would not spend the time in Asia: for he hasted, if it were possible for him, to be at Jerusalem the day of Pentecost."* Here, he keeps it in Jerusalem! Paul tells the Corinthians church to keep the FEAST in 1 Corinthians 5:8—*"Therefore let us keep the feast, not with old leaven, neither with the leaven of malice and wickedness; but with the unleavened bread of sincerity and truth."* So, let's keep the Feasts of the Lord!

Now, back to the Psalms of Ascent (תוֹלָעֲמַה םיִרִישׁ Shirim haMa'alot, Psalms 120-134), which are called such because they relate to the ancient practice of publicly singing these songs when going to God's house in Jerusalem. These poems are connected to תכוס Sukkot, the Feast of Tabernacles, which runs for seven days from the 15th day of the seventh month on the biblical calendar.

Going to the dwelling place of the Holy One of Israel involves going upward in space and thought: the Mountain of God, the Temple Mount. The Psalms of Ascent were connected with going up to the Temple. The male has to make this journey to Jerusalem three times a year, which is called a 'going up,' whether the worshipper came from north or south, east, or west. All of the songs are suitable for use on such occasions. They were occasionally called Pilgrim Psalms by many scholars. The people would dance before the Lord with flaming torches in their hands, and they would sing before Him songs and praises. The Levites would play on harps, lyres, cymbals, trumpets, and other musical instruments beyond counting, standing as they played on the fifteen steps that go down from the Israelites' court to the women's court, corresponding to the fifteen Songs of Ascents.

There is a saying, "If one has never experienced the Feast of Tabernacles in Jerusalem, you have never experienced full joy!" I would agree! I have experienced the Feast of Tabernacles in Jerusalem fourteen times myself! Jesus was at His final Tabernacle celebration while on earth, and Jesus offered to fulfill the anticipated yearnings of many hearts on the Feast Day: He offered refreshment renewal (John 7:37), rejoicing (John 8:12), and rest (John 9:14). I mentioned that the Psalms of Ascent were always sung at night, standing. Look at Psalms 134:1-3—*"Behold, bless ye the LORD, all ye servants of the LORD, which by night stand in the house of the LORD. Lift up your hands in the sanctuary, and bless the LORD. The LORD that made heaven and earth bless thee out of Zion."* STAND AND SING THESE SONGS OF ASCENTS IN YOUR NIGHT SEASON AND WATCH THE LORD BLESS YOU!

CHAPTER 9

THE SABBATH

The Sabbath (from Hebrew shavat, "to rest") is observed throughout the year on the seventh day of the week—Saturday. According to biblical tradition, it commemorates the original seventh day on which God rested after completing your creation. I am not going to debate which day is right, but what is the purpose of the Sabbath Day? Isaiah 30:15—*"For thus saith the Lord GOD, the Holy One of Israel; In returning and rest shall ye be saved; in quietness and in confidence shall be your strength: and ye would not."* The Lord was telling them, "Stop trying to do everything yourself, and come unto Me, and I will give you rest."

Jews begin Shabbat each week with the lighting of two candles, which stand for **"Keep"** and **"Remember."** In so doing, they remember how God rested on the seventh day of creation while also looking forward to the Millennial rest promised for the whole earth. We have to trust Him through faith, knowing that as we willingly surrender to His ways, His pleasure, and His words, we will be saved and made completely whole in spirit, soul, and body. We will not only yield our body/members to His call but also our inward beings: our hearts and our minds. We must completely trust Him and give Him all of our being, inside and out. With Jesus, we can come to the Throne of Grace!

Isaiah 58:13-14—*"If thou turn away thy foot from the sabbath, from doing thy pleasure on my holy day; and call the sabbath a delight, the holy of the LORD, honourable; and shalt honour him, not doing thine own ways, nor finding thine own pleasure, nor speaking thine own words: Then shalt thou delight thyself in the LORD; and I will cause thee to ride upon the high places of the earth, and feed thee with the heritage of Jacob thy father: for the mouth of the LORD hath spoken it."*

Not having our own ways, our own pleasures, and even speaking our own words. The Jews got mad at Jesus for doing the works of His Father, not His own. What they didn't know was that Jesus walked in rest all the time. The Sabbath became a continuous feast to help us enter into that rest.

Jesus, the Son of God, lets us hold fast to our confessions.

For we have not a high priest that cannot be touched with the feeling of our infirmities, but one that has been in all points tempted like we are, yet without sin.

Let us therefore draw near with boldness to the Throne of Grace, that we may receive mercy and may find grace to help us in times of need.

CHAPTER 10

JESUS OUR JUBLIEE

The "year acceptable to the Lord" that Jesus spoke about that day in Nazareth was a reference to a Jubilee Year in the Hebrew tradition. Found in Luke 4:18-19—*"The Spirit of the Lord is upon me, because he hath anointed me to preach the gospel to the poor; he hath sent me to heal the brokenhearted, to preach deliverance to the captives, and recovering of sight to the blind, to set at liberty them that are bruised, To preach the acceptable year of the Lord."*

Jesus quoted from Isaiah 61:1-3—

> *"The Spirit of the Lord GOD is upon me; because the LORD hath anointed me to preach good tidings unto the meek; he hath sent me to bind up the brokenhearted, to proclaim liberty to the captives, and the opening of the prison to them that are bound; To proclaim the acceptable year of the LORD, and the day of vengeance of our God; to comfort all that mourn; To appoint unto them that mourn in Zion, to give unto them beauty for ashes, the oil of joy for mourning, the garment of praise for the spirit of heaviness; that they might be called trees of righteousness, the planting of the LORD, that he might be glorified."*

What is "the acceptable year of the Lord?" This term, which Jesus quotes from Isaiah, is used no other place in the Bible. But the meaning is very clear: It is the "year" in which the FULL plan and purpose of God is accomplished. This "year" being not a literal year, but the full cycle, which is called the FINISHED cycle, of restoration in God's redemptive feast seasons were directly tied into the three harvest feasts or seasons of barley, wheat, and fruit. The three feast seasons and the three harvest seasons not only correspond to each other, but speak of the redemptive plan and purpose of God and correspond to the three resurrections in this: By the time we cycle through the feasts and harvest seasons in Israel each year, we have what amounts to a complete picture of the redemptive plan of God. Thus, it can be said that the outworking of this plan of redemption is, "the acceptable year of the Lord." It is HIS year, and it is acceptable to HIM. Every single point

Jesus lists among the things He came to us is FOR us. There isn't a single thing on the list which takes anything away from us.

In other words, Jesus proclaimed HE was the "Year of Jubilee." This was the year following forty-nine sabbatical years (Leviticus 25). That year the land was to lay dormant, prisoners were to be released, and debtors to be forgiven. "Jubilee" meant a year of rest, a time to rest from labor, a time for grace, and a time to celebrate freedom set forth. The people turned their attention to the reading of the Scriptures. After a scripture from the Law had been read, Jesus then stood up to read a preselected, prescribed scripture from the prophets. The scroll of the prophet Isaiah was handed to Him (Luke 4:16-19). Jesus unrolled it and turned to Isaiah 61:1-2; His voice pierced the silence as He read—*"The Spirit of the Lord God is upon me; because the Lord hath anointed me to preach good tidings unto the meek; he hath sent me to bind up the brokenhearted, to proclaim liberty to the captives, and the opening of the prison to them that are bound; To proclaim the acceptable year of the Lord, and the day of vengeance of our God; to comfort all that mourn;"* He stopped and read no more.

Jesus then rolled up the scroll and gave it back to the synagogue Attendant. At this point, Jesus sat down, before he began to teach from the text. I believe Jesus sat down in Elijah's seat reserved for the Messiah. Everyone's eyes were fixed on Him. The people earnestly waited for Jesus to explain the significance of Isaiah's prophecy about the coming Messiah. Jesus turned to the listening people and simply said—*"Today this scripture is fulfilled in your hearing"* (Luke 4:21, NKJV). At first, the people were relieved by the sincerity of His words. People even spoke under their breath favorable affirmation about Joseph's son. Afterwards, Jesus spoke about His refusal to perform miracles in His hometown, and that He—like the prophets Elijah and Elisha—would be rejected by those listening. Christ's claim that *"Today this Scripture IS fulfilled in your hearing,"* stirred up enmity and wrath against Him. Jesus' identity with Isaiah's prophecy, as the promised Messiah, was astonishing—even blasphemous. Just what was it Jesus was claiming to fulfill? Why were His words so blasphemous? And how had He fulfilled Isaiah's prophecy to proclaim "the year of the Lord's favor"?

Let's examine Christ's claim so we can better understand what He meant when He proclaimed, "the year of the Lord's favor." Jesus was claiming to be something very profound. He was affirming that He had come to liberate His people from sin, just as in the Jubilee year the people were liberated from their guilt, debt, and crimes. In other words, Jesus proclaimed HE was the "Year of Jubilee." This was the year following forty-nine sabbatical years. (Leviticus 25) That year the land was to lay dormant, prisoners were to be released and debtors to be forgiven. "Jubilee" meant a year of rest, a time to rest from labor, a time for grace, and a time to celebrate freedom set forth by God (Hebrews 4). It was a time of deliverance and restoration. The Jubilee demonstrated that everything Israel or we have belonged to God. Jesus was the Master, and we were the stewards of His resources (Deuteronomy 15:1-2). The trumpets were blown on the first Sabbath at the beginning of Jubilee. That day was also known as the "Day of Atonement." While the trumpets were sounded throughout the land, lambs were sacrificed to the Lord in the tabernacle, and later in the temple in Jerusalem. The lamb's blood was sprinkled over the Mercy Seat above the Ark of the Covenant. All of this foreshadowed or spoke of Christ and what He had come to do for us. And what was their inheritance they had waited for? That inheritance was the Lord Himself—Messiah! He had come to deliver them and give them His rest.

Hebrews 4:1-3—*"Let us therefore fear, lest, a promise being left us of entering into his rest, any of you should seem to come short of it. For unto us was the gospel preached, as well as unto them: but the word preached did not profit them, not being mixed with faith in them that heard it. For we which have believed do enter into rest, as he said, As I have sworn in my wrath, if they shall enter into my rest: although the works were FINISHED from the foundation of the world."* IT WAS FINISHED, IN THE HEAVENS FROM THE BEGINNING.

> *"There remaineth therefore a rest to the people of God. For he that is entered into his rest, he also hath ceased from his own works, as God did from his. Let us labour therefore to enter into that rest, lest any man fall after the same example of unbelief. For the word of God is quick, and powerful, and sharper than any twoedged sword, piercing even to the dividing asunder of soul and spirit, and of the joints and marrow, and is a discerner of the thoughts and intents of the heart. Neither is there any creature that is not manifest in his sight: but all things are naked and opened unto the eyes of him with whom we have to do. Seeing then that we have a great high priest, that is passed into the heavens, Jesus the Son of God, let us hold fast our profession. For we have not*

an high priest which cannot be touched with the feeling of our infirmities; but was in all points tempted like as we are, yet without sin. Let us therefore come boldly unto the throne of grace, that we may obtain mercy, and find grace to help in time of need." (Hebrews 4:9-16)

Hebrews 4 speaks of God's rest or Sabbath. God never created the Sabbath to be a burden. To call the Sabbath a burden is a distortion. The Sabbath is not only for the Jews, but a blessing instituted at Creation for all humanity before sin even entered our planet.

"If thou turn away thy foot from the sabbath, from doing thy pleasure on my holy day; and call the sabbath a delight, the holy of the LORD, honourable; and shalt honour him, not doing thine own WAYS, nor finding thine own PLEASURE, nor speaking thine own WORDS:"
(Isaiah 58:13)

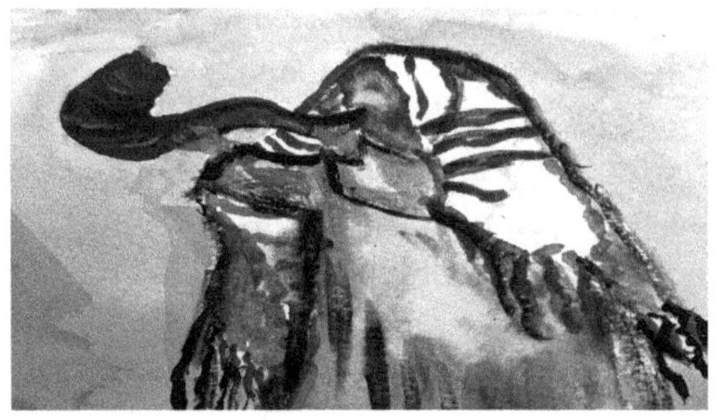

PHOTO ALBUM

Mary Fleenor, my lovely precious sweet Mom!

The artwork found within the pages of this book, and on the following pages of this Photo Album, were created by Sasha Beach.

The Passover Lamb
(Exodus 12:3)
Chapter 1, Page 21

The Lamb for a House
(Exodus 12:3-4)
Chapter 1, Page 22

The Angels in White
(John 20:11-12)
Chapter 3, Page 39

The Barley Sheaf
(Leviticus 23:15-16)
Chapter 4, Page 49

The Day of Pentecost
(Acts 2:1-4)
Chapter 5, Page 63

The "Casting Off" Ceremony
(Micah 7:19)
Chapter 6, Page 77

The Mercy Seat
Chapter 6, Page 79

The Waving of Palm Branches
(A New Day Has Come)
Chapter 7, Page 81

The Water-Drawing
(Isaiah 12:2-3)
Chapter 7, Page 82

The Blind Eyes Healed
(John 9)
Chapter 7, Page 84

The Unleavened Bread
(1 Corinthians 5:8)
Chapter 8, Page 86

We are the Shofar.
The Holy Spirit
is the breath!
(Isaiah 58:13)
Chapter 10, Page 94

www.ingramcontent.com/pod-product-compliance
Lightning Source LLC
La Vergne TN
LVHW010616110826
845149LV00003B/932

* 9 7 8 1 9 6 4 3 5 9 2 7 4 *